Bunny

CHRISTOPHER REEVE

Illustrated by Meryl Henderson

CHRISTOPHER REEVE

Young Actor

by Kathleen Kudlinski

ALADDIN PAPERBACKS

New York London Toronto Sydney

ALADDIN PAPERBACKS
An imprint of Simon & Schuster Children's Publishing Division
1230 Avenue of the Americas, New York, NY 10020

Designed by Lisa Vega
The text of this book was set in New Caledonia.
Manufactured in the United States of America
First Aladdin Paperbacks edition June 2007
2 4 6 8 10 9 7 5 3 1
Library of Congress Control Number 2006939080
ISBN-13: 978-1-4169-1544-7
ISBN-10: 1-4169-1544-3

ILLUSTRATIONS

	PAGE
After a weekend with Dad, Topher and Beejy must walk the last block home to Mom.	4
Appearing in his first play, *The Yeoman of the Guard,* Topher is measured for his costume.	28
Chris flirts with the ballerinas as he works the lights backstage.	45
Chris zips down the mountain in a ski race.	54
Robin Williams, Chris's new friend from Juilliard, jokes around.	81
Chris learns to fly.	90
Chris overdoes it while appearing in *A Matter of Gravity* with Katharine Hepburn.	102
Chris works out for his role playing Superman.	116
Chris on the red carpet with Gae Exton and their children, Alexandra and Matthew.	136
Chris learns to compete in horse races.	152
Chris's wife, Dana Reeve, works with him on rehabilitation after his accident.	184
Dana helps Chris write his book *Still Me*.	194

CONTENTS

	PAGE
Scene Changes	1
Child Actor	17
Cast and Crew	38
Action!	50
The Promise	64
TV Star	85
On Broadway!	96
Superman!	110
Using Fame	124
Jumping New Hurdles	146
Another Promise	163
Superman, Take Two	188
Christopher Reeve Time Line	201
For More Information	205
Acting Credits	207

CHRISTOPHER REEVE

Scene Changes

"Get out of the car."

"Here, Daddy?" Christopher Reeve looked down Wiggens Street. "Aren't you going to drive us all the way home?"

"You're eight, Tophy. You can walk from here. Princeton, New Jersey, is a perfectly safe place. Hold Benjamin's hand."

Topher looked at his little brother. "Beejy has to walk too? Why?"

"Listen here, young man." Franklin Reeve's voice had turned ugly. "I have no interest in seeing *that woman* or her new husband ever again."

Topher felt his little brother's hand find its way into his. "Is he talking about Mama?" Beejy whispered.

"You bet I am," Franklin snarled. "You two had a good week in Connecticut with me. Don't spoil it now."

Topher jumped out of the car. "Thank you, Daddy." He tried to stay close while Mr. Reeve got two small suitcases from the trunk. "I liked the sailing," Topher said, "and the dinner parties and the horses."

"The horses made Tophy's asthma worse," Beejy said.

"But I love them," Topher said, grabbing for his father's hand.

"Franklin?" Mama's angry voice carried down the quiet street. "Don't you dare . . . !"

"Good-bye, boys," Franklin said quickly. He gave each son a squeeze and jumped back into his car. Topher and Beejy stood by their suitcases on the sidewalk as their father's car screeched away.

Mama's heels made a click-clacking sound on the cement walk. "What was *that* about?" She picked up the suitcases.

"Daddy had to hurry," Topher lied. "He had an important meeting."

"Of course he did," Mama said. "Did he and his new wife have much to say about me this time?"

"Oh, yes," Beejy said.

"No, they didn't," Topher said louder. He punched Beejy and tried to change the subject. He glanced at his mother. The sun made her blond hair and blue eyes shine. "That yellow dress looks good, Mama."

She set the suitcases down and smoothed the gathers over her flat stomach. "Why, thank you, Topher," she said.

Beejy punched Topher in the arm.

"Now, now, boys," Mama scolded. "Don't be beastly to each other." She smiled. "Tristam and I have a surprise for you. We'll tell you when he gets home from the university."

She walked them through the gate, up the walk, and across the porch to their side of the rowhouse. "I rode a horse." Topher swung his suitcase proudly.

"I swam over my head," Beejy said back.

"At night, by the bonfire, I made a sand castle," Topher said. "It was huge."

"I squashed it."

"Did not!"

"Did so!"

Both boys tied to squeeze through their front door at once. Mama just laughed.

"Ladies first," she said, and pushed them both aside. "Wipe your feet on the mat." Inside, she put her little yellow hat on the stand next to Tristam's.

Topher sat down on the piano bench and carefully opened the top. He stroked the keys with his fingertips. Mama smiled at him. "You can catch up on your practicing after lunch. I fixed your favorite: Fluffernutters and Ovaltine."

"No thank you, ma'am," Topher said cautiously. He closed the piano and rubbed his stomach.

"Why? I put plenty of peanut butter and marshmallow in the sandwiches. I used soft, new Wonderbread, too."

"Daddy got us a special lunch on the way home," Beejy said. He glanced at Topher and pulled his foot out of the way.

"I should have known!" Mama snarled. "I suppose he got you ice cream cones."

Beejy shook his head. "No, Mommy. We got three-scoop banana splits!"

"Why, that . . . that . . . ," their mother muttered. Topher held his breath, but Mama said no more. She pointed at the door. "Outside now, boys, before I use words you shouldn't hear." Topher wanted to say he'd heard them all already. He wanted to say he understood. He also wanted to cry. "Out," Mama scolded in a quivery voice. She jerked the door open.

Topher and Beejy filed out. Behind them the door closed sharply.

Christopher wanted to punch something. He glanced at the crab apple tree in the front yard. "Bet you can't throw as far as me!" he said. Before his brother could catch up, he'd jumped the stairs three at a time and grabbed a green apple off the ground.

"No!" Topher yelled, hurling it as hard as he could into the street.

"Not fair," Beejy said. "You're in second grade. I'm only in first!"

"Boo-hoo, baby," Topher mocked. He shot another apple, yelling "No!" as loud as he wanted. It felt good. He threw another and another. His muscles burned and his chest heaved. Soon Beejy stood beside him, hurling green apples into the street.

"What do we do now?" Beejy asked. "The apples are all gone."

Topher panted. He still needed to throw

things, to fight. "I know," Toper said. "Let's play pirates!"

"It's 1960, silly. There are no more pirates," Beejy taunted.

Topher didn't answer. Instead he pulled the cellar doors open. He found three big packing boxes left over from Tristam's move into the house. "Ahoy, mate!" he called to his brother. "Let us sail to the top of the world and destroy our enemies."

"Aye, aye," Beejy yelled back. "I'll grab the swords and guns!" He broke dead branches of the hedge along the driveway and raced to meet Topher on the porch.

"All aboard!" Topher ordered. They shoved two boxes together, then climbed into them. "Haul on the mainsail," Topher said. "Thar's a storm ahead!" He swayed left and right to show how rough the seas were.

"First mate is here," Beejy announced. "Look! A bad guy!" The brothers swung swords at the foe. "I got him!" Beejy yelled. He leaned overboard to watch the enemy fall into the water.

"Behind you!" Captain Topher shouted. He ran his sword through another attacker and shoved him overboard. Beejy brought his sword down on a third enemy and Captain Topher drew his pistol.

"Bang!" he shouted. "Bang!" He looked upward. "Haul in the sails. We'll outrun them!" It took all of the boys' strength to pull up the wet sails. The waves grew higher. Topher clung to the gunwales to keep his balance as the boat heaved wildly. "Tie yourself to the mast, my boy!"

"Why?"

"The next wave could wash you overboard!" Captain Topher shaded his eyes and looked into the frothy sea. "Here it comes!" He took a deep breath and held the railing.

Icy water crashed down overhead and

swept the deck. Topher wiped his eyes. His lips tasted of salt. "Beejy!" Topher cried. "Where are you?"

"You knocked me out of the box," Beejy said.

"Swim, Beejy, swim!" Captain Toper called, and heaved the great ship's wheel to the side. "Hold on, m'boy." Tears streamed from his eyes. "Don't die, Beejy!"

The front door opened. "Boys?" Mama called.

Topher stared at the stick in his hand, panting. A heartbeat ago, he'd been holding a sword. He glanced around. He was on his own porch. Tristam was striding up the front walk.

Topher wished he could go back to his pretend world again.

"How are my boys?" Tristam ruffled Topher's and Beejy's brown curls.

"I'm not your boy," Beejy grumbled.

Tristam strode past as if he had not heard.

"And here," he said, "is my best girl." He dropped a grocery bag he was carrying, swept his long arms around Mama, and picked her right up off the ground.

"Ick," Beejy said before Topher stomped on his foot to quiet him.

"Did you tell them, darling?" Tristam asked his wife.

"Boys." Mama waited until both boys were still. "Remember when you were in our wedding last year? You two wore those cute little white outfits?"

Topher froze. *Not again,* he thought. Just looking at himself in the pictures made him cringe.

"Remember how we all promised to be a family that day?" Mama asked.

"And I swore I'd be the best stepfather ever?" Tristam added.

"And he really is, boys, isn't he?" Mama said quickly. "He is such a good father, we've decided to have another baby! It's already on its way." She looked at Tristam. "Next spring you'll have a new brother or sister!" Tristam hugged her extra hard and she giggled. When she had caught her breath again, Mama said, "Isn't that wonderful news, boys?" She spoke to her sons, but she was looking at Tristam.

"Another stepbrother?" Beejy scuffed the toe of his shoe on the porch floor.

The two adults laughed. "No," Tristam explained. "Since you will be sharing a mother, the new little one will be your *half* brother. Or maybe your half sister. Would you like that?"

"I already have two half brothers," Topher said. "And two stepbrothers. They belong to Daddy and Daddy's wife." He thought about how hard it was to get his father's attention. "There are too many people at Daddy's house. I don't want any more here."

"How can you say that?" Mama scolded. "You beastly, beastly boy!" She seemed about to cry.

"Now, Barbara. He just has to get used to the idea, don't you, little man?" Tristam ruffled Topher's hair. "The more the merrier." Topher ducked out from under his stepfather's hand.

"Will he get my bed?" Topher asked. "Will he go to Daddy's with Beejy and me? Will I have to share my toys with him? What about my books?" Questions tumbled out, one after another.

"Later, little man," Tristam silenced him. "Beejy, would you carry my bag inside? I brought us ice cream to celebrate."

Topher watched them wander back toward the kitchen. *"Come back!"* he wanted to yell. He needed answers to his questions. Everything was going to change—again.

At first they had all been happy together, Mama, Daddy, and Beejy, in their home in New York City. He could barely remember that. Then Mama and Daddy divorced. It hurt even to think about. Mama moved to

New Jersey; Daddy moved to Connecticut and married a lady with two older children. Topher squirmed, remembering that wedding. So many people!

Then Daddy and his new wife had little boys. After that, he didn't come to get Topher and Beejy so often. Sometimes it seemed like Daddy forgot about his first boys when he had more. And now Mama was going to have more children too.

Topher sat down on the piano bench and opened the keyboard. He played a scale as loud as he could. Then he played another. He wanted to hurt the keys. He wanted Mama in the kitchen to hear too.

His hands crashed down on the keys, making a horrible, clashing noise. Over and over he played scales, loud and louder. Mama did not come from the kitchen—not even to scold him.

Finally Topher quieted down inside. The scales he had practiced so often came out right now. He began playing in a smooth rhythm, holding his wrists flat and pressing gently with his fingers. Then he looked up at the sheet music his piano teacher had left.

He knew that song by heart now. Could he play it perfectly? Topher began at the top. He focused hard. Every note came out right as he played. The beat was true, too. Topher relaxed and the music surrounded him. He loved this feeling!

When his fingers left the keys, he let the last chord echo in the air.

Suddenly applause broke out in the room. Topher blinked and turned quickly. Mama and Tristam were clapping. So was Beejy! Mama swooped to the piano bench and wrapped her arms around Topher, squeezing tight.

"What did I tell you, Tristam?" she said. "Talent. My Topher has real talent!"

Topher glanced up at the music. Playing piano like that was like playing pirates. It took all his problems away. As soon as Mama let him go, Topher began playing the same song again.

"There, see?" Mama said behind him. "Christopher will be fine with a new baby."

Child Actor

"Do I *have* to change schools, Mom?" Topher set his glass down so hard that milk sloshed onto the dinner table.

"We are sending you to Princeton Country Day School this year," Tristam said. "Beejy will start there next year. You'll both love it."

"How do you know?" Beejy challenged.

"Darling, we have seen it," Mother said. "You are both bored silly in public school."

"But that's where all my friends are," Topher said. "If I change, I'll lose my place on the hockey team. I won't get the fourth-grade teacher I wanted. I'll—"

"Princeton Country Day is where *I* went to school," Tristam interrupted.

Topher shot a glance at Beejy. "That figures," he grumbled.

Despite all his expectations, Topher ended up loving Country Day School. He made friends there easily too. Athletics were important at Country Day, and Topher was a natural at sports. He played goalie on the hockey team and excelled at soccer. He'd played tennis since he was three. Topher made the baseball team, too. Tristam came to every game and cheered for him, almost like a father.

"Call me Tris," he told Topher at the school's father-son carpentry workshop.

"Tris, can you hand me that hammer?" Topher asked without thinking. "Mom will really like this birdhouse, won't she?"

Tristam grinned at him. "We could hang it in the crab apple tree."

"Then we need to make another one"—Topher nailed the roof on tight—"and put it where she can see it from her kitchen window."

"We could give them to her at Christmas," Tristam suggested, "*if* you can wait that long."

"I can wait if you can," Topher teased.

Tristam put an arm around Topher's shoulders and squeezed. For the first time, Topher didn't squirm away.

He didn't avoid the hardest classes at school, either. Topher struggled to get good grades. That was something his father—the real one—really cared about. When Topher got tired of studying for a test, all he had to do was imagine his father's face when he heard his son was on the honor roll. *That* would get his attention!

The other smart students in school liked

Topher because he was such a hard worker. Still, some of the classes seemed almost easy and some of the teachers were boring. One spring afternoon Topher sat gazing out the window in science class. He watched college students practicing soccer on the nearby Princeton University fields. He ached to be running in the field, climbing a rocky cliff, racing in a sailboat—doing *anything* but sitting quietly, hearing facts he already knew.

A knock at the door got his attention. "Pardon the interruption," a tall skinny woman said. "I am from the Princeton Savoyards. We put on plays every year by Gilbert and Sullivan. We're holding auditions now for a few children to appear in the spring play. Does anyone care to try out for a part in *The Yeoman of the Guard*?"

Topher's hand shot up. So did many other hands. "A play about the army!" one boy said.

"Oh, did I mention that you have to be able

to sing well?" the woman added. "This is an operetta."

"An oper*etta*?" another boy said. "Sounds French, like a ballet or something." All the hands came down but Topher's.

"Very well. Come along, young man," she said. As they walked down the hall, she asked about his singing.

"I sing in the junior choir at the Congregational Church," Topher said. "I sing sometimes when I am playing the piano, too."

"You play the piano?" The woman sounded pleased. "That means you read music. You are very tall for fourth grade, and handsome." Topher felt himself blush. "You seem perfect for the part. But rehearsals are held during the day. Some of our performances are children's matinees too. You'd have to miss a good deal of school. Would that be a problem with your folks?"

"No," Topher said. "I'm sure." He knew his mother would be thrilled. She always bragged about how talented he was. Tris was so excited about their new baby, Jeff, that he was saying yes to everything this spring. But Topher's father? None of his other children were in plays. "I really want this part," he told the woman.

"We'll see," she said.

A crowd gathered at one end of the stage in the McCarter Theater. Men and women and a couple of girls chatted nervously. Topher didn't know any of them. He stared up at the bottom of the curtains. They'd been pulled straight up overhead. Walkways crisscrossed beneath the high ceiling. Lights of all colors pointed down from poles, and ropes hung like jungle vines.

"Villagers! Center stage!" someone called out. The crowd began walking out on stage and Topher hurried to follow. He almost tripped in surprise. The stage was sloped downward toward the audience. "Line up downstage!" the voice demanded. Everyone stepped down to the edge of the stage. Because of the lights, Topher could not see anyone clearly in the huge theater. He tried to shade his eyes.

"That's the casting director," the man next to Topher explained.

"Name and age in order!" the director demanded.

When it was Topher's turn, he said clearly, "Christopher Reeve. I'm nine." Then he spread his arms and smiled into the lights.

"Thank you, Chris. *Next*!" the director insisted.

Chris, Topher thought. That sounded more grown-up than his nickname.

"Not bad, Chris. Act confident right away," the helpful man complimented him. "You've done this before, haven't you?"

There was no time to answer—the man at the piano had started playing a song. People passed sheet music down the line. Topher read. The key was high, but that was fine with him. His singing voice was high and clear, and he'd always sung tenor in the choir. He began to hum along with the piano.

As he read the words, he grinned. The song was funny! Around him people began singing along as they picked up the tune. Some of them were loud; others, whispery and uncertain. A few were wildly off-key. The pianist played through the entire song twice, then stopped.

"Osage, the McNamaras, Mr. Jones, please try out for our *next* production." With some laughter and a few groans, those people left the stage. "Now, from the top," the pianist prompted the crowd.

Topher sang out happily. He imagined the theater full of people. They were laughing at the words. Topher shook his finger at one point, because it seemed to go with the song. At the end of that verse, the piano stopped again. The casting director read out a list of names and invited them to leave the stage. Only about a dozen people remained.

Topher stood grinning at center stage.

"Congratulations," he heard. "You will be the villagers. Pick up a rehearsal schedule as you leave. *Next batch!*"

"My Topher! On stage? At the McCarter?" Mom's voice rose as she listened to Topher's news that night at home. "That theater seats a *thousand* people! You're going to be famous! I knew it!" Tiny Jeff began wailing in her arms.

"You hug him, Tris!" Mom said. "The baby . . ."

Tristam's hug squeezed all the air out of Topher. "That's from me *and* your mother," Tristam explained. "Now tell us about your schedule, rehearsals and all." In the end, Topher's parents agreed to allow him to miss school as long as he kept his grades up.

"Thank you!" Topher said gratefully, returning the hug.

They called Topher's dad in Connecticut

for permission. His answer was the same. "So long he makes up the school work."

The next day, Topher rode his bicycle to school early. He waited outside the headmaster's office while the other boys arrived. "What did you do, Topher?" one of his friends teased. "You never get in trouble!"

"I got a part in a play. I'll have to miss a lot of school," Topher said. He wondered if his friend would think the whole idea was stupid.

"Holy cow!" the boy said. "Wait till I tell everyone!" He turned and yelled down the crowded hallway, "Topher is a star! Today, Princeton! Tomorrow, Broadway! Then it's Hollywood, m'boy!"

"Hush. It's just a little part," Topher scolded—but he was grinning.

The Headmaster standing in the doorway behind Topher was not smiling. "Step into my office," he said before there could be any more yelling in the halls. He listened to Topher's plan for making up class time. He pulled the "Reeve" folder out of his files and studied it. He called Topher's mother at home to make sure he had her permission.

"We like to have our boys involved in the community," he said at last. "You seem to be a serious student."

"Oh yes, sir," Topher grinned. He was thinking about how much school he was going to miss just to be in some play.

"Report to the wardrobe mistress," the director said when Topher arrived for the first rehearsal. A tall slender woman told him how to find the costume room.

Topher wandered down the branching hallways until he knew he was lost. He stepped into a room ringing with the sound of hammers. The Beatles played from a radio somewhere and the sharp smell of paint filled the air. "Costumes is three doors down on the

left," a teenage boy gestured with a paintbrush. "We're building the set here." When Topher paused, the boy continued. "Don't worry. Everybody gets lost at first. Stop back when you have a minute and I'll show you what we do here."

The costume room was huge too, and filled with racks and racks of clothing. "Just a minute!" a cheery voice called. Topher looked at the costume sketches pinned to the wall.

"The wardrobe mistress can measure you now." A man grinned at him as he rushed past and out the door.

"This is like dressing up for Halloween!" Topher told the wardrobe mistress, who checked his name off on a clipboard.

"No, it is not," she said. She measured his waist, his shoulders, and his neck. "When the audience first sees you onstage, they know you're just some kid from town. They know you are only pretending to be a villager from a hundred years ago." She wrote his measurements down on a clipboard. "In the first few moments of the play, the audience decides to make believe you really *are* a villager. Your costume and makeup help them pretend along with you. Soon the audience actually forgets you are just a neighbor—unless you wave and say, 'Hi, Mom,' of course."

Topher laughed and said, "I would never do that!"

"But if you pay attention to a baby crying in the audience? An ambulance siren outside? A sudden light or noise or smell? If you lose your place in the script for any reason, it breaks the spell. We're all depending on you to make this play work."

Topher stared at the woman. She meant it. The director, the actors, the teenager painting the set—they all were taking this very seriously. And they were taking *him* seriously too.

• • •

After weeks of rehearsals and a dress rehearsal in full costume, *The Yeoman of the Guard* was finally ready. The actors gathered early to get into costume and have their makeup applied. The lighting crew tested every light. Behind the curtain, the props crew set fake bushes and water fountains around the set. While the audience filled the auditorium, Topher and the others looked at the freshly printed programs. Then they warmed up their singing voices. They did concentration exercises, too, to get past opening-night jitters.

Finally Topher and the other villagers took their places onstage, pretending to be going about a normal day back in medieval times. The orchestra played the opening bars of music and the curtain rose. Over the music, a gasp and some applause went up from the audience as they saw the set. Topher thought his heart would stop, but everyone was moving onstage. He focused on staying in character. He knew where to go, what to say, and when to sing, so he did. He'd even been told when to expect applause and how to just wait a beat for it before going on. But no one had told him how exciting this would be.

Everyone was working together to hold on to the fantasy—and at any minute, it could snap and fall apart. Weeks' worth of effort would have been for nothing. Could they make it work? Adrenaline surged through Topher the way it did when he was sailing in a close race or guarding the hockey goal from a slap shot. He fought the impulse to laugh aloud with the excitement of it. Instead he turned with the other villagers and launched into the next song.

When the play was over, his mother rushed up to him in the lobby. "Topher!" she cried. "You were brilliant!" Topher's father, down for the evening from Connecticut, gave him a warm hug. Tristam clapped him on the back. Benjy wouldn't even meet his eyes.

Before Topher could ask what was wrong, a girl pushed up to him. "Can I have your autograph?" She held out the program. "Right here by your name?"

"Me too! Me too!" Suddenly Topher was surrounded by people asking him to sign their playbills. He looked helplessly at his mother. She laughed and pointed to the door, gesturing that they'd wait for him outside. Topher nodded and went back to his fans.

At the celebration dinner that night, Tristam beamed at Topher. Mama joked about her son, the star. She held baby Jeff's hands and made them clap together. Benjy grumbled something about the *real* stars of the play signing more autographs. Topher sang one of the villager songs again.

But the play wasn't over. Three times that weekend and three the next, Topher got to feel the same rush of excitement. Then the school performances started. For weeks yellow school busses pulled up to the McCaren Theater and the Princeton Savoyards group repeated the play for children. Some days at ten thirty, others at two thirty, Topher would quietly gather his books and walk right out of class. He'd ride his bicycle to the theater, get into costume and makeup, and feel the magic again.

The final show was the hardest. As the curtain fell for the last time, Topher looked around at all his friends, some young, some old. They'd gotten so close over the past three months. When would they see each other again? The Princeton Savoyards would put on another Gilbert and Sullivan operetta next year, but who knew which actors would be chosen then?

That summer Topher visited his father in Connecticut.

"Honor roll?" his father said, slapping Topher on the back. "That's my boy. How is that tennis swing coming?" That night they celebrated summer with a bonfire in the backyard. Benjy and Topher were there, along with their father's other children—Mark, Brock, and Alya, the youngest. All five kids took turns running toward the towering flames. They threw sticks into the inferno. Then they then spun about and ran for cool air.

They all sailed, too. Mr. Reeve was a strict teacher. He demanded excellence—whether it was grades at school, a tennis serve, how tightly the mainsail was pulled in, or how straight his children sat on a saddle. Alya and Brock were becoming great horseback riders. They took lessons near their home in Connecticut. Chris leaned on the fence watching them take jumps. It looked so exciting! "Heels down! Shoulders back!" his father coached from the sidelines. "Attagirl." He turned to his son. "You sure you don't want to ride this summer, Topher?" he asked.

He shook his head. "I'm wheezing already, Dad," he said sadly. "Allergies. Maybe asthma. I'm better off out here. Can we go sailing this afternoon?"

The breeze was rising, just the way his father liked it. It would be exciting out there. His father kept the sailboat heeling way over to grab every bit of force from the wind. You had to hold on tight to keep from falling in. You also had to duck in a heartbeat when his father called, "Ready about? Hard to lee!" The mainsail's heavy wooden boom would swing across the boat, knocking anything or anyone out of its way.

Father skied with the same intensity, Topher thought, leaning on the rail. He could still remember whooshing down the slopes with his father when he was three. It wasn't the beginner slope, either. The speed and the danger were such a rush!

Topher thought suddenly of that other rush of excitement—the one when the curtain comes up. He savored that memory as he watched his stepsister jump fence after fence.

Cast and Crew

"Great save, Chris!" The hockey team crowded around him, slapping his helmet. Chris, now an eighth grader, had outgrown his childhood nickname. He pulled himself off the ice awkwardly. The goalie uniform, all pads and padding, made him seem clumsy—until he was up on his skates. Then he was quicksilver fast and agile. His long arms and legs helped him guard the goal box too.

"You going out for baseball this spring?" one of his team captains asked as they headed into the locker room. "Sure could use you again—our superathelete."

"I bet he'll be trying out for another school play," the forward said. "Remember how he brought the house down last year as a lady?" The boys around him hooted, but Chris smiled as he remembered.

Princeton Country Day's theater group planned to do a murder mystery, *Witness for the Prosecution*, during Chris's seventh-grade year. After being onstage at the McCarter theater, Chris thought he was a good actor, so he auditioned for the big parts. Instead he landed the role of Janet Mackenzie, a Scottish housemaid.

Princeton Country Day was a boy's school. There were no girls to cast for the women's parts. Chris had known that when he tried out. Still, pretending to be a Scottish woman had seemed as awkward at first as wearing goalie pads.

Chris decided to master a Scottish accent

so that he would sound as if he really came from Scotland. He listened to recordings of Scots speaking. He mimicked their words until he could repeat them perfectly. Then he tried to use the same accent on the script he had to memorize for the play,

Janet Mackenzie's big speech came right in the middle of the first act. Wearing a woman's housedress and a wig, Chris delivered her speech with a perfect accent. He made her sound outraged, too, and middle-aged. When he finished speaking, everyone in the theater burst into applause. Chris didn't grin then. He knew better than to step out of character. But it made him smile every time he thought about it.

"You planning to do both?" the team captain prompted. Chris blinked and looked around. He was in the locker room, in his hockey uniform, not standing, center stage, in costume. He struggled to remember what he'd been asked.

"Oh, yeah," he told his teammate. "I'm going to do theater and baseball, too."

"Who do you think you are?" one of the offensive guards said. "A sixth-grade Superman?"

Around them locker doors slammed. "Oh, you know our Chris," the captain said. "He'll probably fit both of those activities in, and be on the honor roll and the debating club, too." Showers splashed on in the next room and the boys hurried to clean up and change.

"Hi, Mom!" Chris called when he got home. Little Jeff was playing with his trucks on the floor. The newest baby, Kevin, lay in a playpen sucking his toes. "Mom?" Chris called again. There was no answer.

When Chris stepped into the kitchen, Ben looked up from his homework. "Mom is taking a nap," he explained. "She didn't sleep so well last night. Tristam didn't come home again." Chris slammed his books down on the counter. Ben shrugged at him and went back to his homework.

Chris poured himself a glass of milk. As he drank it, he thought how worried his mother must be—and how angry. He didn't want to be any part of the scene when Tris finally came home. But where could he go? Chris thought quickly. "If Mom asks, tell her I'm over at the McCarter Theater," he told Ben.

"Did you get another part in a play?" Ben asked.

"No." Chris hurried outside to grab his bicycle. He pedaled to the theater in record time, parked his bike, and stood looking at the stage door. He had no right to be there. No part in a play. No jobs to do backstage. Chris sighed. Probably no one would even remember him.

A pickup truck screeched to a halt behind him. "Chris? Chris! Am I glad you're here!" It was Mike, the teenager from the set shop. Chris grinned. Mike had remembered his name!

"I have to get all this wood into the shop." Mike gestured at the bed of the truck. "You got a minute to help?"

In answer, Chris grabbed a couple of two-by-fours. "Let's go!" he said.

"Hi, Chris!" someone yelled as they passed the costume room.

"Look, Chris is back!"

"How're ya doing, Chris?" Friendly calls followed him down the hall.

"When Mike is done with you, I need a hand," the props manager called to him through another open door.

When the boys set down the load of wood, Mike stared at Chris. "What exactly are you smiling about?"

Chris just shook his head. "There's more lumber to carry in." He glanced at the door. "Time's a wasting."

Soon Chris began riding his bike to the theater every day after school. The crew always had odd jobs to do—carrying, lifting, hammering, painting, or moving. Chris learned new skills. The men in the lighting department showed him how to work the light boards. He learned basic wiring too. He was able to wire the dressing room speakers so actors could hear the play in progress up on stage.

The Princeton Savoyards rented the theater for another Gilbert and Sullivan play. This time, Chris was far overhead working the lights. Ballet companies from Pittsburgh and New York City came to use the stage too. In eighth grade, Chris was very tall and handsome. He loved to flirt with the ballerinas. To show off, he took on the job of raising and lowering the huge curtains. There were counter weights to make it easier, but Chris knew how to ride the ropes. He let them pull him far up over the ballerina's heads. Then, when he had their attention, he would swoop down again.

His hard work and quick mind had everyone's attention. Besides the visiting productions,

McCarter had a professional repertory company. The actors and actresses were paid. So were the directors and stagehand crew chiefs. Others, like Chris, worked for the love and the excitement of theater. Together they produced several plays each season. Often big name actors came to star in shows. From famous stars down to the stagehands, everyone pulled together to make every performance a success.

Sometimes Chris's New Jersey family pulled together too. In the fall, Chris climbed the apple tree in their yard. He picked a bucketful of apples. Then he lowered the bucket by rope. Ben ran the apples in to Mother, who cleaned them and tossed them in a pot. Then Chris climbed down, and Ben took his turn in the treetop. By dinnertime everyone enjoyed fresh applesauce. But Tris often had to cancel family affairs. He said it was business. Chris often felt he couldn't depend on his stepfather.

Chris's Connecticut family acted as a team

as well. On summer vacations, they crewed on Franklin's sailing boat. Sometimes they sailed out to islands, where they had glorious picnics together. Sometimes they entered races. Winter vacations meant skiing and ski races, then hot apple cider in front of fireplaces at the ski lodge. But Franklin wasn't happy with his children unless they had won at sailing or skiing. Chris often felt he couldn't satisfy his father.

The theater was different. In school or at the McCarter, Chris knew people were really glad to have his help. And in eighth grade, he began to get acting roles with the repertory company.

After a successful opening night of the play *Finian's Rainbow*, the director, a visiting professional from New York, praised Chris's acting.

I could be an actor, Chris thought. He loved the idea. He could always have the excitement, always have the close working friendships, always have the applause. Now that he had gotten professional encouragement, it seemed more than just possible. Within the week, Chris had changed the dream to a goal. "I *will* be an actor," he told himself.

But Chris was realistic. Many people wanted to go into show business. Most of them never did more than high school plays. Some of them grew up and volunteered in community theaters. For them it was a hobby. Chris wanted to earn his living as an actor. More, he wanted to be a *star*. Chris decided to do everything in his power to reach his goal.

Chris stared at the bulletin board backstage at the McCarter: SUMMER THEATER WORKSHOP IN LAWRENCEVILLE. Lawrenceville was just ten miles from Princeton. The tryouts for the workshop were next week!

"You know it will mean studying indoors all summer?" his mother reminded him.

"Sounds good," Tris said, "but don't you want to get a job and earn some money?"

"Do they award you a certificate?" Franklin demanded to know.

To all of them, Chris's answer was the same. "There is no better way for me to learn about the theater right now," he said. "Besides, I'll be making contact with people who can help me become a star someday."

His parents looked at each other and smiled, but they gave him their permission to audition for the workshop.

Action!

"Happy fifteenth birthday, dear."

"But, Mom," Chris stammered. "A piano? My *own* piano?" He ran his hands along the glossy wood. He sat on the matching bench.

Kevin climbed up to sit beside him. "Topher, can I play?" he asked.

"Me too!" Jeff demanded.

Ben, as usual, had his head in a large math book.

"Maybe someday," Chris promised. He opened the keyboard, spread his large hands over the keys, and began playing. "Oh," he breathed. The sound was, by turns, rich and full, crisp and mellow, changing as he pressed the foot pedals. He tried playing church hymns. He shifted to a jazz number. Kevin and Jeff wandered away toward the playroom. Chris played a classic full of crashing chords, then a lighthearted ragtime piece.

"This piano makes me sound so good!" he said, looking up at his mother.

"It's all your practicing that makes you sound this good," she corrected him. "We thought you needed an instrument that matched your talent."

Chris looked over at Tristam standing in the corner. "Thanks, Tris," he said. Chris had to admit that his stepfather was generous. He had bought this huge new house for them in Princeton. He paid tuition for Country Day School. Tris had paid the fees for the summer theater workshop. He drove him to Lawrenceville ever day over the summer, too. Tris supported whatever sports and school activities either of his stepchildren wanted to do. But by ninth grade Chris knew Tris was drifting away from his mother—and that wasn't fair. Hadn't they all promised to be a family forever?

Stop worrying, he told himself. There was enough going on in the world, that sometimes he lost himself in worry. The war in Vietnam. Hunger. Pollution. Civil rights. And there had been all the assasinations: President Kennedy, Martin Luther King, Robert Kennedy. And riots, too. It didn't seem fair to be rich and white and safe in beautiful Princeton. But Chris didn't know what else to do.

He threw himself into the arts. At school he starred in plays and worked on the literary magazine. At church he sang with the choir at every service. He had started a band with a few of his school friends. In the community he helped with all the productions at the McCarter Theater.

• • •

"And how are your grades?" Franklin asked when he saw him at Christmas break.

"Honor roll, Father," Chris was proud to say.

"There is a special gift for you in the guest room," his father announced. "No peeking until we are just about to leave."

"We're leaving?" Chris looked around at his father's huge new home in Higganum, Connecticut. "But I just got here."

Franklin laughed. "We are all going to the ski lodge. I've entered all my children in the big race—and that includes you."

Christopher carried his suitcase up to the guest room and gasped. The Christmas present was a set of racing skis tied with a little bow. Next to them sat a pair of ski boots. "No peeking," he said to himself, and laughed. Now he couldn't wait to get out on the slopes.

"I expect each of you to win," Franklin said as they sorted out the arm bands with their entry numbers. A fluffy snow fell on the

mountainside. Chris pulled on his number and looked around at the competition. They were mostly other high schoolers like him. A few wore ski team jackets. Only one was as tall as Chris.

Alya led her class. So did Mark and Brock, Franklin's other children. Ben had stayed home in New Jersey for a conference on computers, so only Chris remained. His class began with a blistering run by a team member from Vermont. The next skier wiped out near the finish line. Two competitors made fine runs but could not beat the first skier's time.

"That was a course record for your age group," Franklin told Chris. "Worth trying to beat, but no shame if you don't win this one." Chris just grinned at his father. With these new skis and perfect weather conditions, nothing could stop him. At last it was Chris's turn.

His body hummed with adrenaline just

from looking down the slope. Chris planted his ski poles, breathed lightly, and imagined winning. When the starter's pistol went off, he heaved against his poles and lunged downward. His skis were close but exactly parallel, soaring across the surface of the powder. The wind whipped past his face, tearing his breath away. Chris tucked even tighter and leaned into a bend. He felt wild laughter rise in his throat. He'd never skied this fast before. He tucked deeper for more speed.

The finish line was upon him before he expected it. He turned sharply, digging the edges of his skis into the soft snow. He leaned to the side to force the turn. It was like heeling over on the side of his father's sailboat. He pushed until he *had* to fall over, but the speed and curve held his body just off the snow. It sprayed a plume of snow over all of the onlookers. Finally he slowed, stood, and bowed to the crowd, grinning and panting.

"You're first by a mile!" Alya thumped him on the back. "A course record!"

"He could have broken his neck," someone said from the crowd.

"Daredevil!" another voice called in disgust.

But Chris just grinned. "Alya, as soon as the event is over, let's race again, you and me." Alya laughed and threw a snowball at him.

"I'm not that crazy," she said, but there was admiration in her voice.

"Nice job," Franklin told everyone that night at the dinner table. "Five more days of skiing—if some of us don't end up in the hospital." He looked directly at Chris. "You took too many risks today, you know."

Chris swallowed. He never seemed to be good enough for his father. Franklin went on. "We need to talk about racing season on the water. We could use you this summer, Topher—*if* you can control yourself."

Chris cleared his throat. "I'm not sure

I can crew for you, Father," he said. "I've applied to be an apprentice at Williamstown Summer Theater. It's at Williams College in Massachusetts."

"Theater?" Franklin sounded stunned.

"Only sixty kids from around the country are chosen." Chris said. "And I really think I have a chance to get in."

Chris was right. He arrived in Williamstown just a few days after school was done in June. The summer theater kept him so busy, it seemed he never stopped running. The apprentices ran the sound system, hung the lights, painted the scenery, and worked on costumes. They tried out for parts, too—real parts working with professional actors.

There were only a few Equity actors in the troupe. They were people who had worked for pay enough times to join the professional Actor's Guild. Eight plays were planned for the season. That meant there were more roles than the professionals could handle.

The apprentices were invited to audition. Chris never missed a chance to try out. It meant acting with some of the best known actors of the time. He could learn from the director, Nikos Psacharopoulos, too. During the winter the famous Nikos taught acting and directing at Yale University.

Seven times Chris auditioned. Five times he got a part. Now his parts were not all as "extras." In *The Yeoman of the Guard*, Chris had been an extra, part of a crowd with no lines to learn. At Williamstown he landed small but important roles where the audience focused on him as he spoke his lines.

He also performed in a cabaret. That was a show the actors and apprentices put on for local dinner crowds. There was singing and dancing, comedy, and drama, too. Everyone had a chance to audition with their greatest talent. They all had time in the spotlight.

It was hard work. The hours were long.

The Williams College dormitories were noisy social places twenty-four hours a day. The summer apprentices were soon exhausted. Many of them quit. Not Chris. To him it was as thrilling as downhill skiing. All summer long he was just hours away from curtain time on some stage with some show. Everything had to be ready. Lights, actors, costumes, makeup, sets, props, music—it was always a scramble to put it all together.

The teens who stayed all pitched in to work together. The Equity actors helped each other and shared their knowledge with the apprentices. The director treated the teens as adults.

"I *love* this!" Chris told an actress after their third curtain call one night.

"There's no business like show business," she quoted the famous song. "Now, Chris, when you take a bow, pause to look at your audience. They were part of the success of the play, too, you know. Meet their eyes and smile. When you bow, you are bowing to *them* to thank *them*. They will applaud twice as hard—and might even give you a standing ovation."

Scraps of advice like this flew from every direction during the summer. Every morning started with a voice class where apprentices learned to project their lines throughout a theater. They practiced singing in ways that protected their vocal chords. They learned breath control and how to put feeling into their singing. Other classes taught how to move onstage. There were even classes on how to be a director.

There was no time off at all—and Chris loved it that way. He did not have time to think about the situation with his father or with his stepfather. He did not worry about the war in Vietnam—or anything else except the next show. Long before his ninth-grade summer was over, Chris knew he'd be coming back the Williamstown Summer Theater. He had finally found a place that felt like home.

During his eleventh-grade summer, Chris was hired by the Harvard Summer School Repertory Theater in Cambridge, Massachusetts. He earned forty-four dollars a week to work on stage crews and act in several of the summer plays. His rent at a college dorm was nineteen dollars. That left twenty-one dollars for food and entertainment. Having to skimp on food and make due without most luxuries seemed just right. Chris felt like a traditional "starving artist." That was how most actors began their careers. But few got as much encouragement as Chris did.

Reviewing his performance in one play, the critic for the *Boston Globe* newspaper said he was "startlingly effective."

The praise rang in his ears for months. He *was* good enough to make it, he thought. As the school year swung around again, he found a teacher just as demanding as Chris was. One day in Mr. Packard's class, a boy made some excuse for skipping class. Chris had performed in a play the night before. He was exhausted, but he was there. He never skipped out. Mr. Packard said, "The only excuse for not attending my class is quadruple amputation." Chris almost gagged but Mr. Packard wasn't done. "In which case, they can still bring you to class—in a basket."

Everyone laughed at the picture, but it was uneasy laughter. Some of them had never thought about amputation before. Quadruple? That meant four. They all tried to imagine what it would be like to have their arms *and* their legs gone. Somebody would have to carry you around. It couldn't really happen, could it?

The scolding wasn't aimed at Chris, but he remembered it for the rest of his life.

The Promise

"I am so proud of you!" Chris's mother brushed a piece of lint off his high school graduation robe.

Chris looked down at her and grinned. "I couldn't have done it without you, Mom," he said. Around them, dozens of high school graduates were saying the same sorts of things to their parents.

Tris wandered over to shake Chris's hand. "You've done well," he said. Chris glanced away from his stepfather. Tris had moved out of the big house in Princeton. Now all four boys lived alone with their mother there. *Another failed marriage,* Chris thought.

"I have to go and line up now," he said, excusing himself.

"It's our famous actor!" the boy behind him in line said. "I suppose you are going right to work on Broadway?"

"Yeah, a pro like Chris?" The student in front of him turned. "He'll earn a million dollars with that union card before the rest of us finish freshman year at college."

Chris laughed. "It's not a union card. It's an Actor's Equity card. It only means I can audition for paying parts in any professional theater—it doesn't mean I'll *get* the parts." He paused. "Besides, I promised my mom I'd get a college degree. I'm going to Cornell, in upstate New York. It's too far from New York City to get to auditions easily, and I won't be tempted to do community theater. I'm just going to be a college student."

Just then, the music started and it was time for the class of 1970 to graduate.

Cornell had a top-rated theater department. That was one reason Chris had agreed to study there. The classes were no harder than anything at Princeton Day School, and Chris was soon getting top grades. He made friends. He joined clubs. He had hours to argue with his friends about the Vietnam War, civil rights, and saving the environment. But he was bored without the excitement of the theater.

Finally the first play of the year, *The Good Woman of Setzuan*, was announced. The director, a theater professor, hung up the schedule of auditions. Students gathered around to read the list of roles. "I just want to be an extra," a freshman said. "I'm not ready for a real role yet."

Chris just listened.

"The seniors and graduate students will

get all the leading parts," a freshman girl remarked. "We'll have to work our way up to the top, just like in high school. I'm going for one of the smaller roles. Maybe I'll get it."

Chris wasn't going to let the fact that he was a freshman get in his way; he decided to go for it. He auditioned for the lead—and got it. Now college life was perfect. He had classes by day and rehearsals every evening. The director had new ideas about how to stage the play and how it should be acted. Chris was learning new techniques as he performed.

Another professor directed the next play. His ideas were entirely different. Chris had a smaller part this time, but he got to absorb another set of tricks. They made the play come alive with energy.

Soon Chris had a chance to act in Shakespeare's famous play *Hamlet.* The director made the entire cast study the play. He assigned homework. The actors and actresses had to read other plays from Shakespeare's time. They had to learn about the history of *Hamlet*. Then they all had to discuss what they had found.

This professor stuck to Shakespeare's words exactly as written. He allowed no new interpretations. No new ideas. The students were tired of the play long before the curtain came up. Chris thought it showed in their performance. By working with these different directors, Chris learned to see drama as an exciting, living experience instead of a dry study of literature.

Since the beginning of the year, Chris had been reading the arts section of the *New York Times* and theater magazines. He got to know the big names, not only of famous actors, but of their agents.

No actor could keep track of all the plays, TV shows, and movies going on around the country. It was a full-time job just to memorize scripts, prepare for roles, and perform them. But when a play finished its run, actors needed another job to pay the bills. They needed help.

Theatrical agents spent all their time finding jobs for actors. They kept track of audition dates and times. They got to know the directors and what each one was looking for in an actor. *Someday,* Chris thought when he read about agents, *someday I'll have one.* He shooed these thoughts away, remembering that he'd promised his mother to finish college first.

Early in his freshman year, Chris walked back into his dormitory after a Monday morning class. He stepped into the house mother's office. "Any mail for me?" he asked.

"Yes, dear," the grandmotherly woman said. "A letter from home and a fancy one from New York." She held it up close to her thick glasses. "It's from a Stark Hesseltine. Is he a relative?"

Christopher swallowed hard. Stark Hesseltine was an agent. He had discovered

Robert Redford while the actor was still a student. He represented many famous actors and actresses. What did he want? Chris tucked the envelope into a pocket and hurried upstairs to his room.

He put the mail on his desk and stared at it. *It's probably a form letter,* he told himself as he tried to breathe slowly. *Maybe every theater student gets one. "Get in touch with us when you graduate," it'll say.*

There was another slim possibility. This famous New York agent wanted to represent him, and now. What would Chris do then? He had made a promise to his mother.

It took two days for Chris to work up the nerve to open the letter. "I saw one of your recent performances," Stark Hesseltine had written. Chris's heart stopped as he read on. "I would like to represent you. Could you come to my office in New York City sometime soon so we can talk this over?"

Before the week was over, Chris drove five

hours to get to the city and walked into Stark's office at Creative Management Associates. "Hold all my calls," the agent told his secretary. Then he looked Chris up and down. "Well," he said, "you're too tall for movies." He gestured to a chair. When Chris sat down, Stark asked, "When are you available?" It almost sounded like Stark had an acting job ready for him immediately.

"Well, I made a promise," Chris began. He knew he might lose the chance to work with this top agent, but he explained why he had to stay and finish college first.

"Your mother is a smart woman," Stark said. "I remember my own days at Harvard. Why don't you come down to the office once a month? I'll see if we can't get you connected with the right casting directors. We'll get you a summer job to really start your career."

Once a month Chris drove five hours to his agent's office and five hours back to campus. With Stark's help, Chris auditioned for—

and was offered—parts in major movies and plays with big stars. Then Cornell scheduled its final exams. Chris had to refuse the parts that would cause him to miss finals. The only role left was a play. It would pay all of Chris's expenses plus the percentage Stark charged for finding the job. Chris toured all over New England that summer with the production and reported to Cornell just before classes started again.

As a sophomore, Chris could take more interesting courses: acting, voice, and history of theater, as well as math and French. He performed in school plays and drove down to see his agent every month. This time, Stark connected him to a project that really excited Chris. The San Diego Shakespeare Summer Theater wanted him to play important parts in several plays throughout the season. But once again, it conflicted with final exams.

Chris went to the head of the university and explained his problem. He offered to make up work and take the exams early. His grades were good. Everyone in the college knew him from plays in which he'd starred. He was even on the school's winning sailing team. The college president knew he might lose a valuable student if he made Chris decide between taking this job and staying for finals. He let Chris go early. "But you have to write all your papers, take the finals, and pass the courses," he said sternly.

Chris had played in Shakespeare's *Hamlet* freshman year. It had seemed a bad experience at the time, but it taught him how to handle difficult Shakespearean language. This summer, he got to die onstage as King Edward the Fourth in *Richard III.* The part was important and he loved the action. When he was given the role of Fenton in *The Merry Wives of Windsor* he was disappointed; the role was bland compared to his turn as King Edward. Of course he dressed in costume every night, went onstage, and said the lines, but his heart wasn't in it. Chris found the role boring.

"Your Edward is acceptable; your Fenton is a mess," the artistic director told him. The director, Ellis Raab, was an old friend, so Chris could ask him what he meant. Ellis explained why Chris had lots of fun pretending to be royalty dying a terrible death.

"You are nothing like Edward," Ellis said. "You made big, simple changes in how you sounded, moved, and acted to bring him to life. Fenton was harder," Ellis explained, "*because* you are more like him. You and Fenton are just regular people. You didn't take the time to find something interesting and original about Fenton. You didn't make tiny, careful changes in your actions to show him clearly to the audience. Chris, you did not *act.* You just wandered out as yourself and delivered his lines. A mess."

Chris thought about it. Ellis was right. There

was more to acting than he had ever thought. Chris had an Equity card and an agent, but suddenly he felt like a beginner onstage again. Now he knew what to work on.

At the end of the summer, Chris didn't want to go back to school. He couldn't imagine sitting in biology or history classes when he had just made such a breakthrough in acting. He had saved up a lot of money from his summer wages. He contacted Cornell. They agreed to give him half a year off to study acting on his own.

With a backpack and a map, Chris headed to England. For months he visited theaters in Scotland and Ireland, England and Wales. He went backstage and helped the crews. He talked with the actors. He watched classic plays like Shakespeare's and newly written plays, too. He watched the audiences to see how they reacted.

Chris ended up in London, where he went to dozens more plays. He got to know the actors.

"My American accent is not quite right," one

of them confessed. "Would you help me?" Chris worked with the entire cast, teaching them how to speak like an American. Sometimes he wrote out part of the script with American sounds instead of British ones. "Laboratory: You call it a 'la-bore-a-tree,' we call it a 'lab-rah-tor-ee,' " he wrote. Other times he read an actor's part to him. He even sat on a stool in front of the whole cast once, reading a newspaper aloud. His help made the play sound far better.

After London, he went to France. Theaters were different there. He studied for weeks backstage and from the audience. It made him long to be onstage. He spoke so much French, he began to feel French. He had been wandering around long enough to wish for a regular schedule again. He'd met hundreds of new people, but he missed his old friends. Chris was homesick.

He arrived back at Cornell just in time for the second semester to start. Chris was glad to be home among familiar people and accents, food and politics. That feeling didn't last long. He had to sit for hours in history classes. He had to take tests and exams in physics class too. "I will never use physics as an actor! Why am I wasting my time here?" he complained to everyone who would listen.

The casting director who had hired him to work at the San Diego Shakespeare Summer Theater had an idea. "I am teaching now at the Juilliard School in New York," Jack O'Brien said. "It is one of the three best acting schools in the country. Could you transfer here for your senior year?"

Chris explained the idea to his parents and the Cornell school administration. It took a while, but he talked them all into it. Now all he had to do was get into Juilliard. He knew that two thousand students applied to their acting program every year—and only twenty were accepted. Only two or three were admitted to the two-year-long advanced program Chris wanted. He knew he had far more experience than most students. He had receive good reviews on his acting. His grades were good. He got a recommendation from Jack O'Brien.

The only thing left was his audition. Chris spent weeks choosing pieces from two plays: one classical, and one modern. He rehearsed them for hours. When his turn came to audition, Chris walked calmly onto the stage. He took his time clearing away chairs that another student had left behind. He knew how important it was to seem relaxed and in control when auditioning. Then he went into character and did his first piece. It was intense and angry, sad and thoughtful. He paused and breathed quietly when that was finished. He shifted easily into the lighthearted character of his second piece. Chris put everything he had learned about acting into his performance, and then it was done.

"Thank you," he was told. "Next!" He had

to get out of the way so another student could audition.

Chris went back to Cornell and waited.

Three weeks later a letter arrived: "Congratulations. Report to Juilliard on September 15." It told him that he and only one other student had been accepted into the advanced program. The other boy was named Robin Williams.

Robin had more energy than anyone Chris had ever known. And he was funny. He spoke fast and thought faster. Most of the other students simply teased along with him, trying to keep up with Robin's manic sense of humor. Chris joked with him, of course, but sometimes, late at night in their dorm room, Robin and Chris just talked. They shared dreams and fears. They discussed professors and movie stars, grades and girls. They talked about world problems. "What can we do to solve them?" Chris worried.

Robin knew what he meant. They were so rich compared with most of the world's people. They got to study at a top acting school. Many people never even learned to read. Chris and Robin wished there were something they could do to help.

They became best friends. All of their classes were together. Acting. Movement. Voice. Directing. Dance. Improvesation. They learned and grew and laughed together. Going anywhere with Robin was an adventure. One night Chris went with him to a lobster restaurant. "You'll have to wait for a table," the waitress said. "Please stand in the line out there by the lobster tank."

Chris saw Robin's eyes twinkle. All he could do was wait to see what mischief Robin had in mind. It didn't take long. Robin Williams pushed both sleeves up and plunged his hands into the lobster tank. He pulled out two lobsters, their claws waving wildly.

Some people screamed. Others scolded.

Soon everyone was laughing wildly as Robin made up a story on the spot. He used the lobsters like puppets. The animals dripped onto the carpet and sprayed water on the crowd. Nobody minded. They were all gasping for breath and trying to keep up with the wild humor Robin spun.

"Sir," the restaurant waitress said. *"SIR!"* When Robin finally turned to her, she said, "Your table is ready." The crowd applauded as Robin thanked the lobsters and returned them to their tank. Then Chris followed Robin past people who'd been waiting even longer to be seated.

After performing his first role at Juilliard, Chris was called in to see John Houseman, the director of the drama department. Chris felt he'd done a fine job as Dr. Johnny in *Summer and Smoke* by Tennessee Williams. What did Mr. Houseman want? He had been known to expel a student on the spot for a bad performance. "It's not worth our time to train you," he would say. "Good luck!"

This time the message was different. "Mr. Reeve," he said, "it is terribly important that you become a serious classical actor." Chris froze at the man's solemn words. Then John Houseman smiled. "Unless, of course, someone offers you a . . . load of money to do something else." Now Chris smiled. Houseman went on to offer him a great honor. "We'd like you to join Juilliard's acting company."

Chris thought fast. This was Juilliard's graduate program. It meant being on a bus, touring America, and performing for twenty-six weeks. It would mean missing the wonderful classes in New York City. It might change his agreement with Cornell. What if he couldn't graduate?

"No, thank you," Chris had to say. He finished the year of classes and plays, deepening his friendship with Robin, and networking with other young New York–based actors. Just for practice, he auditioned for all sorts of roles. He tried out for movie parts, stage leads, and even a daytime TV series. He earned full credit for a year's classwork and graduated with a degree in theater from Cornell.

Chris wanted to go back to Juilliard for another year for a master's degree. When he told his mother and stepfather about his wishes, he got a surprise. "With my other children coming up to college age," Tris told him, "I can't afford to keep paying for you to go to school." He paused for a moment, then said, "Sorry."

TV Star

"What am I going to do, Stark?" Chris asked his agent. "I want to finish another year at Juilliard, but I have no money."

"You need a part-time job," Stark Hesseltine said, tapping a pencil on his desk. "Remember your audition for the TV series?"

Chris did. "*Love of Life*," he said, remembering the series title. "But that was just a soap opera."

"Its good, steady work for an actor, Chris. The pay is good, too. And you'd develop a fan base."

Chris shook his head in disbelief. "Nobody takes those seriously, do they?"

Stark spoke to the *Love of Life* producers. They wanted Chris to play the role of a handsome bad boy, Ben Harper. They were willing to arrange things so he would only need to be filming two days a week. They'd make sure he was done by midday, too. Chris talked with John Houseman. Juilliard would work around his schedule. Even part-time, his pay would cover Stark's agency fee, Juilliard's tuition, and his living costs, with money to spare.

Many of his professors warned him that his career would be over if he worked on a soap opera. They told him he would never be taken seriously as an actor again. Chris needed the money. He decided to prove them all wrong.

Chris started filming in July. Soap opera work was hard. Every afternoon he was given a script to memorize by the next day. It was often twenty-five pages long. Before, he'd always had weeks to learn his lines and he knew how the story would end. Now he never knew what would happen to his character next because the writers were plotting out the story as it was broadcast.

Filming was nothing like live theater. There was no audience out beyond the edge of a broad stage. Instead huge cameras whooshed around on quiet wheels. They followed him, rolling closer and pulling away. His words were picked up by microphones hanging from enormous booms right over his head. Electrical cables snaked everywhere on the floor and stagehands stood right at his elbows. A large monitor showed what the cameras were recording.

The cameras kept rolling unless someone made a big mistake.

Then the director could stomp in, saying "cut!" The filming would stop. The director had to explain what he wanted them all to do differently. Then he would bark, "Take two!" and the scene would have to be started again.

Sometimes the camera came up within inches of Chris's face for a close-up. The more romantic a kiss, the closer the camera came. It sometimes rolled right between Chris and the actor to whom he was speaking.

Of course, none of this clutter showed on the TV screen. Chris couldn't let it show in his acting, either. He had to ignore all the distractions. He had to stay in character. He had to hold a mood, no matter how often it was interrupted. He had to recite his newly learned lines as if he were actually Ben Harper. It was exhausting to hold that level of concentration.

It might not have been easy—but it was fun. Chris was working with professional actors and actresses. He enjoyed the pressure and the excitement of a new production every single day. Chris loved his character. Ben Harper was slick and sneaky. He had married *two* women. One was sweet, the other wicked. Ben flirted with everyone else too. Ben was a crook, so Chris had dramatic action scenes. There were fist fights and arguments, tender scenes and lots of kissing.

The viewers of *Love of Life* sent mail and made phone calls to the station. "We love Ben!" they said. "Give us more of him!"

By August, the series writers made Ben into a major character. Chris was filming five days a week instead of two. He earned far more money. He forgot about finishing his degree at Juilliard. He was too busy being an actor.

Filming daytime TV gave him weekends off. He was done filming by lunch many days. When most actors were working onstage, Chris had free time. He went to plays, of course. He slept in. He ate out. But Chris longed for excitement. He signed up for flying lessons. Within a few months, Chris had his pilot's license. He was making enough money to buy his own plane, a Cherokee 140.

Chris loved the thrill of flying. Adrenaline flooded his body as he did loops and rolls high

above the ground. This was far wilder than sailing or hockey. His plane tore through the sky faster than any downhill skier ever raced. This sport was truly death-defying. If he made a mistake, Chris knew he would crash and die. He made no mistakes. Every time he landed, Chris trembled with the excitement of cheating death.

Flying brought Chris beauty too: sunsets, rainbows, snow-covered mountaintops, cloud fields. Everything looked different from the cockpit of a plane. The sky above was so clear, the stars so bright.

Down on earth, Chris learned what it meant to be a star.

"There he is!" a woman whispered loudly in a restaurant.

Chris looked around to see who she was talking about.

Now a whole table of women were staring at him. "It's Ben Harper!" one of them squealed. "Oh, can I have your autograph?" Even after he signed their napkins, the women watched him eat. They giggled when he went to the men's room. They stared at his date and whispered about her clothes. As he left, one of them called out, "We love you, Ben!"

People recognized him in line at the bank. They asked for autographs when he went out to buy a newspaper. He was noticed in the subway, on the sidewalk, and at stoplights. It was impossible for him to hide. Chris stood six feet four inches tall. He was so handsome, it was startling.

If he was rude to a fan, the soap opera magazines reported it. They printed photographs of him out on dates. Chris couldn't wear sloppy clothes around town or do anything embarrassing. The fans would find out about it. Being Ben Harper was only a job, but it affected all aspects Chris's life.

Most viewers forgot he was a regular guy. They confused him with nasty Ben. "I can't believe what you are doing to your wife!"

women would often say. The men who recognized him said things like, "Go with Arlene. She is *so* hot!"

Once, when he was driving through New Hampshire, Chris stopped for an ice-cream cone. The day was beautiful. Chris sat on the hood of his car in the sunshine. He was licking the cone when a woman darted toward him.

"How *dare* you treat your mother that way!" she shouted. Then she hit him, hard, with her purse.

At twenty, Chris had become famous. And it wasn't all good.

He was a well paid working actor. That had always been his goal. But Chris missed the live stage. There was no applause in television work. No audience. Nobody laughed at his jokes or cheered for his successes. In the studio there was only silence, the whirring of cameras, and the confusion of cramped, tiny sets.

In his time off, he auditioned for plays. Chris had always done that "just for the practice."

Now his acting had improved. He often was offered roles. He agreed to take jobs whenever he had the time.

It was exhausting to tape the soap opera in the day and do a play in the evenings, but Chris felt it was worth the strain. He learned from every experience. In one play, he appeared as a Nazi officer. He thought it would be best if he acted stiff and mean and heartless. The director had other ideas.

"You are already big and strong looking," she said. "Try acting against type."

Chris had heard the term but never tried it. "Your body says one thing," the director explained. "Power. The audience already knows that Nazis were evil. They will see your size and your uniform and expect one thing. If you act warm and earnest, it will startle them. You will be far more chilling."

Chris tried the technique. He played a truly evil man who seemed nice. The audiences loved him.

That play, like many, was only scheduled to run a few weeks. When the run was over, he auditioned for other plays. Chris did not always get the parts he wanted, but he didn't let rejections stop him. Instead he pushed himself to try harder. Chris was already successful in the soap opera. He wanted more. He aimed to be a world-famous actor. Chris knew he'd have to fight for that prize.

On Broadway!

An exciting rumor passed among the young actors that Chris knew. The legendary actress Katharine Hepburn was going to come out of retirement. She would perform in a new play called *A Matter of Gravity.* Kate was world famous after many successful movies. She had starred in some of the best plays on Broadway. People loved her for her looks, her skill, and her attitude. All those fans would come to see her perform once again. That made this new play a sure hit.

Kate was going to play the lead, a grandmother. Someone would have to play her grandson. Whoever got that part would be instantly famous. Chris decided to try out.

He didn't stop to wonder if he would have time to be a soap opera star and a Broadway actor, too. He could not pass up the chance to work with a genius like Kate Hepburn.

Two hundred actors tried out for the role. Kate watched every audition, waiting to see her perfect costar. When Chris walked out onto the stage to try out, the theater was dark. He could not see Kate, but he knew she was watching. Chris tried to connect with the great actress. That sometimes helped an actor get a role.

"Miss Hepburn?" he called out. "My grandmother says she went to school with you at Bryn Mawr. She sends her greetings." Chris waited a moment to see if Kate would answer.

"Oh, I remember Bea," the actress called back. "I never did like her much."

Chris's mouth went dry. He wondered if he should just give up and go home. But he really wanted this part. The try-out scene was a meeting between Kate's character and her grandson. Chris had memorized the lines and practiced his presentation. He looked around the stage.

Chairs were scattered here and there. A tired-looking man slouched in one. "I'm the stage manager," he said. "I'll read Miss Hepburn's lines to you." He started reciting in a flat tone.

No! Chris thought. *Not this way.* "Help me move the chairs," he told the manager. Surprised, the man got onto his feet. Moving about, he seemed to take on energy. Chris had taken control of the audition. They acted through the scene. It went just as Chris had planned.

"Rehearsals begin September seventeenth," Kate called from the darkness.

Chris could not believe it. He had landed a part in a Broadway play! Stark couldn't believe it either. "What were you thinking?" the agent sputtered. "You can't take a job that starts in September 1975. You are under contract to act in *Love of Life* until July of 1976. How are you going to hold two major jobs for eleven months?"

"I've managed to juggle plays and the soap opera before," Chris said.

"Broadway plays are different," Stark said. "Sure, your rehearsals will be right here in New York. But the play will be tried out in other cities first. Philadelphia. Boston. New Haven. Even Toronto, Canada! The producers watch how audiences react in these towns. They change the script and the setting—the direction, too. Only when it is perfect will they bring it to Broadway."

"I'll work something out," Chris said. "I have to."

For the rehearsal month, life was easy.

Chris had no problem learning his lines to play Nicky. Just in case he got sick, another actor rehearsed for the Nicky part. An extra actress learned all the grandmother's lines, too. These understudies were ready to step in if anything happened to Kate or Chris. "The show must go on," Kate insisted, "no matter what." Sixty-seven-year-old Kate bossed all of them around. Chris didn't mind. It was like having a cranky professor who was also a friend.

Once *A Matter of Gravity* moved out of town, Chris really had to scramble. He performed the play every evening in some city or other. Then he could only sleep a few hours. At dawn Chris caught a train for New York City. He learned the day's soap opera lines on the way. In the city, he taped the show. Then Chris got back on a train. It always arrived just in time for him to rush to the play.

He was learning from everything. He was

gaining extra fame. He was earning plenty of money. But Chris had no time to relax. He had no time to sit down and eat meals. Mostly Chris just grabbed a candy bar and hurried on. He thought he could go on forever this way. He was wrong.

His entrance in act one was dramatic. Kate stood downstage, busy being an old lady. Chris, as her grandson, was supposed to burst through the doors center stage. "Grandmother!" he would cry. Then he rushed across the stage to fold her in a big hug.

One night while the play was in New Haven, Chris burst through the doors. He cried out, "Grandmother!" just like he was supposed to. Then he fainted. Chris bounced off a table and fell flat on the stage, unconscious.

The audience thought perhaps he was supposed to do this. Before they realized he was out cold, Kate Hepburn turned to them. "This boy's a darn fool," she announced. "He doesn't

eat enough red meat." Then she called for the curtain to be brought down.

Stagehands carried Chris back to the dressing room. A doctor came in just about the time Chris woke up. "Exhaustion," he announced. "That and malnutrition. He'll be fine if he gets some rest and starts taking care of himself."

The show had to go on. Chris struggled to his feet. "I'm all right now," he told Kate.

"The understudy will fill in for you tonight," she said firmly. "You are just lucky you are a little bit better actor than he is. Otherwise I'd fire you here and now. I need somebody with more sense."

Chris promised he would take better care of himself. For once, he had to sit out the play. He had to listen to the applause from backstage—applause that should have been his. It was only one of the many lessons Kate taught him.

"Be fascinating," she said once. "Always

be fascinating." It took Chris a while to see what she meant. "If you're playing someone who is a drunk," she explained one day, "show him sober sometimes." Another time she said, "Show the contradictions in each character. Be unpredictable." That was who she was. Sometimes she acted gruff or insulting, then she would turn suddenly warm and caring. Chris never knew what to expect. And he did find her fascinating.

Every night he watched this legend work with him onstage. She acted in a way different from anything he had ever tried. She always appeared to be Kate Hepburn. She acted by making changes on the *inside*, not by changing her outward appearance. Chris watched and he learned.

At last the play opened on Broadway in New York City. KATHARINE HEPBURN, the sign said on the theater. It was in bright lights above the play's title. That was fine with Chris. He knew people would come just to see her.

Chris's name came farther down, below the title name. He stood on the sidewalk gazing up at it. Someday his name would be above the title too. But he was only twenty-four. There was time.

Chris's mother came from New Jersey on opening night. His father drove down from Connecticut. Both of his stepparents came too. They all sat in the first row. Chris kept peeking at them through the curtain. He never thought he'd see them together.

"Places!" the stage manager whispered. Chris had to hurry back behind the doors, center stage. The curtain went up. Everyone applauded at the sight of Kate Hepburn onstage once again on Broadway. Then Chris threw the doors open. "Grandmother!" he cried, and the play began.

Afterward his whole family joined him backstage. Chris introduced them to Kate. They all looked happy and proud—even Franklin. Chris felt like he was flying. He had made it! For an actor nothing was bigger than a Broadway show. And his family was together too, talking to one another again.

A Matter of Gravity played on Broadway over a hundred times. The theater sold out every seat. The producers were happy because they were making money. They were ready to put the show on six days a week for years. But after eight months the crowds thinned. Some seats stayed empty. The money stopped flowing.

"We're going to close here at a hundred and fifty performances," the stage manager told the cast. "We'll be taking the play to Los Angeles. You all need to move with us or start making other plans."

The news hit Chris hard. He did not want to leave New York, but a change made sense. He wasn't getting great reviews in *A Matter of Gravity.* Kate got all the attention. That made sense, but Chris was tired of performing in her shadow. He thought about television. He wondered about movies. Chris yearned for something new and exciting.

He quit when the play moved from New York. His contract at the soap opera had ended and they had killed off his character, so he couldn't just reappear in the series. For the first time in years, he was facing unemployment.

The years of hectic schedules had taken their toll. Chris was exhausted. He didn't think he could face another round of auditions, not after he'd been at the top of the profession. Was this all there was?

He got into his plane and flew to California. He had money to last for months. He needed to rest. He needed to heal. Chris spent time worrying about his life. What good was he doing, really? Chris sat on the beach, stared at the water, and thought. He flew his Cherokee 140 east to the desert and swooped over its still spaces, thinking.

Stark knew Chris would need another job someday soon. He called other agents in the film and TV business in Hollywood. He asked them to keep a lookout for jobs that fit Chris's talents. Stark let Chris know what they found.

There were a few auditions that interested him. Chris tried out for parts in TV series. He even landed a starring role in *The Man from Atlantis*. It sounded good until he learned the details. He would have to wear green contacts and huge fake webbed feet. That would be a bad move for someone trying to make a name as serious actor. He said, "No, thank you," and went back to staring out over the ocean.

The next audition led to a small role in a big movie, *Gray Lady Down*. He spent the summer filming on navy ships out in the Pacific Ocean. His character took part in the fake rescue of a submarine. He had a good time filming.

The reviews of the movie were terrible, though. Chris knew this was no way to further his career. He got into his plane and flew back to New York City.

Superman!

When Chris returned to New York in October, he called several friends. One of them, William Hurt, was starring in a new play. *My Life* wouldn't be playing in one of the big flashy theaters on Broadway. It was a smaller, off-Broadway production. A major part in the play was still open. Bill Hurt got Chris an audition.

Two weeks later rehearsals began. Chris played a grandfather. He was also Bill's understudy. For one evening, he got to play the lead. Otherwise he was happy working again before a live audience. He would have been happy to stay there, but a call from Stark changed everything.

"Chris, my boy," he said. "Hold on to your hat. A major motion picture studio just called." He gave Chris a moment to catch his breath. "Now, this is a long shot, but the casting director really seems to want you."

Chris wrote the details down: Saturday. Three o'clock. *Superman, the Movie*.

"It's going to be a big-budget movie," Stark said. "Nobody has seen a script yet. You might as well go talk to them."

"It will be good practice," the two said together, and laughed.

Chris talked with the director and the producer in a plush office. They talked about his experience. They discussed his age, twenty-four. He posed for them in the light by the window. They compared names of friends in the business. They mentioned that a world-famous actor had been hired to play

Superman's father. Another superstar would play Lex Luthor, the bad guy. Their names alone made the movie a sure hit. The conversation ended two hours later.

"I honestly don't know what they thought of me," Chris reported to Stark that evening.

The next morning, there was a knock at Chris's door. When he opened it, a messenger stood outside. "Please sign for this," he said, then handed Chris a heavy package. It held scripts for *two* Superman movies. Over coffee, Chris scanned through three hundred pages of action, dialogue, and stage direction.

The screenplay was wonderful! It was true to the comic book story that everyone loved. It had humor, too. And it had a character Chris knew he could handle. This Superman was all-powerful. This hero would be perfect played against type. Chris could project humility and gentleness while looking like a superhero.

Chris flinched. He was awfully skinny to

play a superhero. Perhaps, he thought, there was a costume that would give him muscles. Chris read the last page and sat back, grinning.

At eleven o'clock, Stark called. "You really impressed them," he said. "Get this: They want you to fly to London right away for a screen test."

That night Chris told everyone in the cast of *My Life* his news. They were all excited for him. "I can take over your part," his understudy said. "Can you give me a week to get ready?" The director agreed to let Chris go. This was the kind of chance every actor dreamed of getting someday.

"I won't get the part," he told his friends. "Look at me. I'm a stringbean." He looked around the room. "I'll bring everybody something cool from London, though."

"Good luck!" They cheered for him as he left the next weekend. The producer had sent Chris airplane tickets—first class. On the long transatlantic flight, Chris thought about Clark Kent and Superman. The actor George Reeves had played them almost the same on a recent TV Superman series. There was no secret. Clark Kent was clearly Superman and Lois Lane seemed pretty stupid not to notice.

Chris decided to play the two men very differently. With his eyes closed, he imagined the characters. Superman stood tall, his arms crossed over his chest. His voice was deep, confident. Clark Kent stood slightly stooped. His hands stayed in his pockets. He shifted his weight from foot to foot. His eyes flicked about, nervously. His voice was higher and thin.

That was too simple. "Be fascinating," Kate Hepburn had told him. Chris tried to think of an unlikely characteristic for the men. It might be interesting if the confident superhero had no experience with women. He would be shy about unexpected things.

And Clark Kent? Could he have a sly way of flirting—perhaps with his eyes? Or be clumsy? Chris spent hours in thought. By the time he arrived in London, he was ready.

Chris performed the scenes he'd chosen. He used every trick he'd learned in school or onstage. "Thank you" was all the producer said when he had finished. Chris walked to the dressing room and changed. He stepped out of the studio building and climbed into a limousine for the trip back to his hotel.

The driver leaned over the seat and grinned at Chris. "I'm not supposed to tell you this," he said, "but you got the part."

Before any filming began, many people helped Chris get ready.

"Now do another thirty reps." Chris's trainer showed him no mercy. "You have to bulk up enough to fill out the leotard. Tomorrow we'll add more weight." Seven days a week Chris worked out. "Don't stop." "Keep breathing."

"You're sore? Good!" The trainer kept after him for hours. It showed. Within weeks, Chris began bulking up. His biceps swelled. His neck thickened. Still, the trainer pushed him.

Props people fitted Chris for harnesses. They hooked him up to wires. Stunt men showed him how to hang steady on the wires but seem to be flying. The takeoffs and landings were the hardest parts. Chris practiced to make them look natural and easy.

The wardrobe crew worked double-time with Chris. He was, after all, two characters. His Clark Kent costumes were simple. They looked like standard men's suits from the 1930s. Superman was harder. Chris had dozens of skintight costumes. They had no pockets. No zippers showed. No sweat was supposed to show either. Whenever a damp spot appeared under Chris's arms, on his chest, or around his neck, filming came to a stop. Everyone waited while he changed into a new, dry Superman suit.

The wardrobe people made several Superman capes. Some hung softly from Chris's shoulders. Others were starched into stiff ripples or folds. Those were for flying scenes. On camera, they seemed to be rippling in the wind.

Chris's own hair was curly and brown. That had to be fixed. The comic book Superman had black hair with a curl on his forehead. Makeup people dyed Chris's hair black. They trimmed it carefully. Hairspray made it stay in place. The curl on his forehead was stiff with gel.

While the crews were getting him ready, Chris was rehearsing his scenes. His leading lady was Margot Kidder. Her Lois Lane character sometimes had to react to Chris as Clark Kent. In other scenes she had to play to his Superman. Between takes she was just herself, talking with plain old Chris Reeve. Being all these people seemed awkward at first. Soon the two were laughing and teasing.

Once again, bright lights, overhead sound booms, crew members, and huge cameras moved about the stage. Chris was used to ignoring them. It was harder when filming on the street. One day, between scenes, he backed up and stepped on the toes of a beautiful young woman walking by. Her name was Gae Exton, and she was a famous model. He blushed, apologized, and asked her out to dinner. "No, thank you, Superman," she said with a grin. They exchanged numbers, but she was busy. Not only did she work as a model, but she was an agent for other models too. Chris called and kept asking. Soon they began dating.

For *Love of Life*, he had acted straight through each scene. The director seldom yelled "cut!" Movie timetables were very different. One day Chris might do a scene from the end of the film. The next day the director could ask for something from the middle. Some days Chris heard "take two," then "take three," and repeated his lines right through seven takes before the director was satisfied. No matter how tired he was of it, Chris had to project exactly the right mood for the scene every time the director yelled "action!" He had to jump right into character and remember his lines. He could not look tired or impatient.

Despite all the hard work, Chris was having a good time. *Superman* was a fun movie. The script had lots of funny parts and the crew and actors were friendly. There was a lot of joking around on the set—until the director yelled "action!"

Many times that action took place high in the air. Chris spent a lot of time dangling in his harness. Sometimes he hung from a truck ladder. Other times he hung from huge cranes far above the New York streets. In one scene, he fought with a burglar who had climbed a skyscraper using suction cups. During the filming, a crowd gathered in the street below.

They cheered wildly for Superman. Chris knew then that the movie was going to be a hit.

In one scene he had to rescue a cat from a tree. It took a full day for the filming. First the cat wouldn't cooperate as Superman whooshed by on his wire harness. Take after take, the cat got more frightened. Chris worked up a sweat. He had to change clothes. The cat scratched at him. They replaced the cat with a stuffed animal. The harness tangled in the tree.

All the while a young boy watched from his seventh-floor window. "Hello, Superman!" he called out.

"Cut!" the director yelled.

At lunchtime, the boy called, "Do you want some spaghetti, Superman? My mom said it would be okay if you came in the window."

The director was laughing too hard to yell "cut." As the afternoon went on, Superman swooped back and forth by the boy's window.

Chris saw the child do his homework. He watched him climb into bed in his pj's. "Good night, Superman," the boy called at last.

"Cut!" the director yelled.

Finally all the cameras were turned off. Miles of film were gathered. The movie had been shot all out of order. Many scenes had been recorded over and over. Now it was time for the film's editors to look through it all. They snipped out the good parts. They spliced them together in order. Then they added music to it. This process took months.

While they got the movie ready, Chris had some time off. He flew his Cherokee 140 in great loop-de-loops over the ocean. He raced aboard his father's sailboat. Chris tried hang gliding. He rode the rapids. He started dating Gae Exton, the model he had met while filming *Superman*. Chris fell deeply in love with the leggy blond. Everything added to the excitement of waiting for the movie to come out.

The studio publicity people worked overtime. They set up interviews for Chris with newspapers and magazines. They got him on radio programs. His face appeared on posters and cereal boxes. Superman made the cover of *Time* magazine. By the time the movie came out in December of 1978, everyone in America was wild to see it.

Huge crowds waited in lines at movie theaters. They cheered aloud for the new handsome American hero. Reviewers watched the movie too. They wrote such good things that even more people came to see Superman. Chris could not go anywhere without fans greeting him.

"There he is!" they'd squeal. "Ooooooh—a real movie star!"

Using Fame

Soon Chris and Gae fell in love, and he asked her to move into his apartment. "As long as I can still work on my career," Gae said. The paparazzi snapped photos of Chris and Gae on the red carpet for newspapers and magazines. They made a great couple, but they didn't talk about getting married. Chris had watched his mother and father's marriage go bad. Then he had watched Tris's marriage with his mom fail too. They all ended up deeply hurt. Chris loved Gae too much to put her through something like that.

They had plenty of money from his work on *Superman*. Invitations to parties arrived daily. Chris was also getting many offers to star in movies. Often it was for action films. Chris did not want to be cast as one superhero or another for the rest of his life. He said no to hero roles. He said no to other big movies, too. He was waiting for the perfect script.

The Make-A-Wish Foundation called Chris. They told him about a little boy who was very sick. "He wants to meet Superman before he dies," they said. "That is what our foundation does. We find ways to make sick kids' greatest wishes come true."

Chris wore his costume and cape when he showed up at the child's bedside in the hospital. He almost cried when he saw the look on the boy's face. Superman stayed and talked all afternoon. Then he offered to visit with other children for the Make-A-Wish Foundation.

Newspaper photographers always met him on the way out of hospitals. Chris didn't mind their questions or the blinding flashes from their cameras. He just wanted to talk about the wonderful Make-A-Wish Foundation. Within days, donations always flooded the foundation offices. That meant they could afford to make many more kids' wishes come true.

Chris saw how he could use his movie-star status to do good. He knew he couldn't help everyone, though. Chris looked into many charity foundations. At last he chose to join the board of Save the Children. This organization collects money to feed hungry children around the world.

He posed for pictures, wrote letters, and showed up at their ceremonies. Because he was Superman, Chris helped Save the Children raise many thousands of dollars. He felt better about himself than he had in years.

He even volunteered to be a track and field coach for the Special Olympics in Brockport, New York. Every one of the children he worked with had a special challenge. Some of them used crutches to run; others had to stay in their wheelchairs. Chris could not believe their courage. No matter what obstacles life presented, these kids just kept trying.

Chris could not imagine being handicapped. He had always been healthy, handsome, athletic, and rich. It seemed unfair that he had been so lucky. He wasn't dying in a hospital, starving in a poor country, or struggling in a wheelchair. At least now he had found ways to share his luck with others.

Chris starred in a movie called *Somewhere in Time*. He thought it would be a great success. His name went "above the line," sparkling over the top of the movie title. That was the kind of respect Kate Hepburn got. Now it would be his, too, Chris thought. But when the movie was released, Chris was struck by a terrible surprise: The film bombed. Chris was crushed. He'd never failed so badly at anything before.

He did not have much time to mope, though. Chris and Gae moved to England to film the second Superman movie. Much of the story had been filmed when *Superman* was being shot, but several new scenes were needed. Chris had gained thirty pounds of muscle for *Superman*; by now most of it was gone. He needed to get his hero bulk back, and quickly. Chris spent his days filming, and his trainer kept him busy in the evenings.

A new director had been hired. He used two or three cameras all at once. If one didn't catch the right light or angle, another camera probably did. That way, the filming went faster.

Gae's modeling career was going well, and they were still both in demand at parties. Their lives were happy and busy. Soon Gae announced that she was pregnant. Chris and Gae were going to be parents!

The night Gae went into labor, Chris took her to the hospital. He stayed with her all night, but the baby still hadn't come. After waiting for hours and hours, Chris told Gae that he'd scheduled an important business lunch that day. He didn't want to miss their baby's birth, but it didn't seem like the baby was going to come anytime soon. They checked with the nurse and she said it would be hours before the baby appeared.

"Go ahead, Chris," Gae said.

As dessert was being served at the fancy London restaurant, a waitress rushed to Chris's table. "The hospital called," she said. "The baby is coming!"

Without another word, Chris bolted from the table. He caught a cab and sped across London. He burst into the hospital room just as his little boy was born. "Here he is." Chris handed the child to Gae. "Matthew." He often told his friends this was the most wonderful moment of his life. He was twenty-seven.

Within months they had finished shooting *Superman II*. Chris, Gae, and Matthew, and their live-in nanny, flew back to the United States. They rented a house in Los Angles, California, where Chris spent his time playing with Matthew and reading scripts for movies. There were no roles he liked. Chris loved family life, but missed the stage. He bought a bigger plane and went to all the parties, but nothing compared to the thrill of the theater. Chris started making calls.

The director at Williamstown Summer Theater was glad to hear from Chris. "Of course you can come back. I'll put you in a play or two this summer," he said.

Chris and his family moved back east to Massachusetts. The theater cast and crew were glad to see him. Chris loved the excitement of rehearsals and opening nights. Here there was no chance of replaying a scene. It was like walking a tightrope. Any misstep—by anyone—and the illusion would come crashing down. Chris was delighted to be hearing the applause again. This, he knew, was pure theater.

Chris's friend Robin Williams came to see his performance. Robin stayed for days, enjoying the theater and the quiet countryside. The old friends had only met for dinner now and then in New York or in California. In Williamstown they had time to talk.

They both felt it was time they started doing something to make a difference in the world. They decided to pull together a group with other famous friends in the acting business. Word spread and the group started to grow, but they still hadn't decided what cause to support. Their fame gave them a lot of power—any issue they took on would be covered by the press, worldwide. Chris had shown that with Save the Children and the Make-A-Wish Foundation.

"We'll be the Creative Coalition," someone suggested. They all tossed in their ideas for action. Fighting homelessness? Protecting the environment? Cleaning up the election system? They all agreed that these were worthy causes, but the artists found there was an issue that truly united them all. The government had a committee called the National Endowment for the Arts. It had huge amounts of money and gave funds to help American artists. Most theaters, painters, museums, orchestras, dance companies, and writers did not make much money. If they did original work, they could apply to the NEA for a grant. Thousands of these grants, from a few hundred dollars to thousands, let artists continue producing art.

One artist produced photographs with money from one of these grants. The photographs bothered a congressman who didn't think it was art at all. He felt the government shouldn't be supporting this type of work. He called for an end to the entire NEA. That would mean that thousands of artists would be out of business. Hundreds of schools, museums, and festivals would have to close their doors.

The Creative Coalition went to work. Chris testified in Congress. He called his senator. He met with congressmen. Other Coalition actors did, too. They gave speeches. They wrote editorials. They argued that America's art and artists were a national treasure. Because they were famous, the press took up the Coalition's cause. The angry congressman did manage to lower the NEA's funds, but he did not destroy the National Endowment for the Arts.

The Coalition did not limit its work to the United States. In a South American country, Chile, a group of actors were arrested. Their crime? They had played scenes that mocked the government.

The United States Constitution protected actors. Here people are guaranteed free speech. Chris himself had acted in plays with antiwar messages. He had challenged the stockpile of nuclear weapons; he had complained about the treatment of wounded veterans. His actions probably bothered some people, but they made others think. But Chris would never be arrested in the United States. He would not be killed. Art, like plays and movies and TV shows, was protected. So were the artists.

In Chile there was no free speech. Seventy actors had been rounded up and thrown into jail. They all were sentenced to death for treason.

The Creative Coalition wasted no time. Anyone who could break away flew to Chile. They gathered with hundreds of others in front of the courthouse, the National Palace, and the jail. Chris protested, marching with a sign. He did not have to tell anyone he was Superman—as soon as someone recognized his face, they told the press. Reporters swarmed around him. They found every famous American actor in the crowd. They took pictures and quotes from this American Creative Coalition. Within hours, newspapers around the world printed the photographs. Articles were written and news broadcasts scripted. Soon everyone knew about the death sentence for the actors. The Chilean government was embarrassed by the publicity and decided to let all the actors go.

Chris came home with the rest of the Coalition members. They were giddy with relief. They had exercised their power and actually saved lives. Now they had to get back to work onstage or in front of cameras. All the way home they thought of other causes they could help. Chris knew he was part of something really big—and really good.

In the fall, *Superman II* came out. Chris's name was above the line. Again there were red carpets and magazine articles. Again people flocked to the movie. Some of them said it wasn't as good as *Superman*. Others said it was better.

The producers said they wanted to do *Superman III*, because no matter what, it was

a surefire way to make money. Chris agreed only if it had an antiwar, anti-nuclear-weapon story line. He had always worried about global peace. Chris had talked for hours about his beliefs with his high school buddies, with Robin Williams, with Gae. Now, he thought, he could have Superman do his talking for him. Think what a difference he could make!

The movie was not very well reviewed. Worse than that, it was not well attended.

Chris kept spending the summers at Williamstown. He and Gae had bought a house there. But he flew off to film movies more and more often. "It will be easier on you and Matthew if you stay home," he told Gae.

"Would you be willing to take over the lead role of a Broadway play?" Chris's agent Stark was on the phone.

"You know that depends on what the play is," Chris answered. Stark described *The Fifth of July*. The play was about a real person, Ken Talley. He had been a lively schoolteacher before he was drafted into the army. He was sent to fight in Vietnam. His legs were hurt there when a bomb blew up. Both of them had to be amputated. The play takes place when he gets home and has to deal with his new life from a wheelchair.

By the time Stark was finished talking, Chris knew he would say yes. Here was another chance to spread his antiwar message. It would be a real challenge to play a man so angry—and so handicapped. It would prove that he was a serious actor. It would put Chris back on Broadway, too.

To prepare to play Ken, Chris went to a veterans hospital in New York. Mike Sulsona agreed to coach him. Mike had been in Vietnam too. Both of his legs had been blown off. The veterans hospital had given him false legs and taught him to walk again.

Mike taught Chris how to stand up and sit down like an amputee. Chris learned how to walk like Mike and how tiring it was for him to do every action. He learned Ken's lines for the play perfectly. Most actors would try to do exactly the same thing every single performance. Chris decided to act the play "in the moment" instead. As soon as he got into character, Chris began feeling Ken's emotions, not his own. Onstage, Chris did not do everything as rehearsed. He let Ken's feelings tell him how to say a line or how to move, how long to pause or when to smile.

Of course Chris wore leg braces during the play to keep his "real" legs from moving. He had to concentrate not to wiggle his toes. Fake toes never move. Any motion would remind the audience that Chris and the rest of the cast were just pretending.

Chris's name was above the lights, and on Broadway. Reviewers all praised his "natural" performance. Audiences stood to applaud him every night. Chris was thrilled. This proved he wasn't just a strong guy in tights and a cape. He was a classical actor.

The next time Chris said yes to a movie script, it had an even more challenging role. In *Deathtrap*, he played a mentally twisted student who was a cold-blooded murderer. Many of his fans were shocked to see him in this role. No one complained about his acting, though. He was chilling and he was believable.

Over the next few years, Chris played many good roles. Some were onstage. Others were in film. He traveled all over the world for his work. When little Matthew was four, Gae had another baby. This time it was a girl. Chris was halfway around the world, filming in Yugoslavia. He hurried home to see Gae and meet little Alexandra. Within days he had to go back abroad to finish the film.

"Al!" Chris would call when he got home. "Matthew!" They would run in from the swimming pool to hug their father. Chris loved the hugging. He tussled with his children on the carpet. He rolled down grassy hillsides with them. He threw them up into the air and caught them for more hugs. He taught little Matthew to ski when he was three. He showed Alexandra how to swim almost before she could walk. Whenever Chris was in town, he was the perfect loving father. But he was cooler with Gae. They had never married. Now they didn't think they ever would.

Then the producers talked Chris into making a fourth Superman movie. Gae and the children moved with Chris back to their home in England for the filming. The script was full of clumsy lines and tasteless jokes. It made Chris look like a terrible actor and he knew it. When the film wrapped, Chris knew immediately that he had made a mistake. He told the producers he would never act in another Superman movie. He fired his long-time agent, Stark.

At this time, Chris's relationship with Gae ended as well.

"I want to see the children as much as I can,"

he told her. "And I promise I will support you and them for the rest of your lives. But I can't live with you anymore."

Then he left his family in England and flew home to New York. He wandered the snowy city streets, falling into a depression. Some friends took him to sunny Barbados, in the tropics. Even there, he was grief stricken. He flew a plane. He went scuba diving. He sailed beautiful boats on the turquoise sea. Nothing helped. He came home to his Williamstown house. It was cold and empty, but he began working to fix it up.

Superman IV came out. It was so bad that people wondered if Chris cared about his career at all. Right then, Chris didn't care about much. Luckily his new agent found him interesting jobs. He hosted a documentary for the Smithsonian Institution about the future of flight. He played small roles to keep money coming in. None of the films were hits. Chris had lost his place "above the line" on the credits forever. Once he had been an A-list actor, but now he was sinking to B-list fast.

He appeared in a film shot in Toronto. That was where Gae's brother lived. She brought the children to visit during their spring vacation. She stayed in her brother's apartment. That way Matthew and Al could play with Chris at his hotel. They swam together in the pool and wrestled on the carpet. They explored his trailer on the movie set. They snuggled together, watching cartoons on the hotel bed. Then the children went home to England.

Chris went back to his house in Williamstown. Now he wanted it finished before fall. His two youngest brothers came out for the summer to help. It was nice to have family there. With their energy around, things were not so lonely. And progress was beginning to show on the house.

The director at the Williamstown Summer Theater Festival made sure Chris had work there. Rehearsals went smoothly. The cast worked well together. Chris heard the sound of applause again. He began to heal inside.

He called his children often. They would be coming to visit in July. He was excited about seeing them. He felt happy enough to go out for a drink now and then after the show.

One night he sat with friends in a bar waiting for the show to begin. A group of artists performed there every night. In a cabaret like this, each performer did something different. Some sang. Others did comedy acts. Sometimes scenes from plays were acted out. Jugglers, magicians, and acrobats might take their turn on stage. "Tonight we have a real treat," the announcer said from his tiny stage. He waited for everyone in the bar to get quiet. "May I introduce the world-class actress and singer Dana Morosini." Chris had never heard the name. He sipped his drink and glanced toward the stage.

A young woman came out. She had an honest face and sky-blue eyes. She took control of the stage like a pro. Chris could not take his eyes off her. When Dana began singing, her voice was low and mellow and pure. Within moments, Chris knew he was in love again. It terrified him.

Jumping New Hurdles

The children, Matthew and Alexandra, moved into Chris's house for a month. Three-year-old Al brought her saxophone from England. In the afternoons Chris played the piano along with her. They all swam in a nearby pond. They rode horses together. They played miniature golf with Dana. They watched her sing in the cabaret. Dana and the children grew fond of one another.

Chris was just beginning to feel better. He did not want to deal with love again. He and Dana tried staying just friends.

That didn't work. A strong bond was forming. Like Chris, Dana was a daredevil. She loved dangerous sports like sailing, flying, skiing, and diving. She lived for the thrill of the stage, just like Chris did. Chris was sure he wanted to spend the rest of his life with her—but he was afraid. This seemed too good to be true.

As the year progressed, Chris acted in many plays and took television work. He had to travel for all of the jobs, but he always returned home to Dana. Sometimes Dana traveled with him. They rode horses together for days when he was on a shoot in Yugoslavia. In the summer Chris acted in Williamstown again. Dana moved in with him there. She acted in plays with Chris. When his children came, they felt like a family—almost.

"I can't just keep being your girlfriend," she finally said. "It is not fair to me. It is not fair to Matthew and Al, either."

Chris went to see a therapist. He talked about how his parents had hurt each other and all of their children. "Marriages do *not* have to end that way," the therapist said. "True, that was all you saw as a child. But you do not have to make the same mistakes your parents did." Over the winter, the therapist helped him see how to have a healthy marriage.

Dana and Chris got married on April 11, 1992. They lived together in Williamstown—unless one or the other was on the road for their careers. Matthew and Al visited often. The new family made its own traditions: pillow fights and long horse rides, singing and music, wild sports and quiet cuddles.

To prepare for one of his many film roles ten years earlier, Chris had to ride in a steeplechase. That meant a galloping race over hills and streams. There were fences to jump, too, and trees to avoid. Chris had always done all of his own stunts. He figured he could do this, too.

Extras had been hired to ride in the scene with him. All of them were members of the Hungarian National Equestrian Team. The speed and danger of riding huge horses in a steeplechase left Chris breathless. He wanted more. He watched the team compete in a test that combined training in three areas. First each man put his horse through a complicated pattern of starts and stops, turns, reverses, walks, trots, and canters. They were not allowed to speak to their horses. They had to sit silently in the saddle. They gave their horses commands by squeezing their knees or moving the reins a tiny bit. This silent "dressage" looked like magic.

Next was an all-out gallop across the countryside. The horses jumped fences, leaped over streams and ponds, scrambled up and down little hills, and swerved around trees. "Cross-country" looked like a steeplechase, but it was even faster.

In the last part of combined training, the horses had to jump a series of high gates and hedges all inside a fenced-in area. The animals never got going very fast in this "stadium jumping." There wasn't room for that. It seemed as if they floated up and over the jumps.

Not only did the horses have to compete in all three areas, sometimes they had to do it in *one* day. Dressage came first in the morning. Horses ran the wild cross-country race early in the afternoon. Stadium jumping lasted into the evening. Chris breathed hard, just watching. He *had* to learn this sport!

Whenever he could, he took lessons. The nearest trainer to Williamstown was across the Hudson River, in Bedford, New York. Chris was glad to make the drive. When he and Dana were thinking about building a new house, they chose Bedford. The schools were good. It was near the summer theater—but it held no memories of Gae Exton. Better still, Chris could ride very day. To keep his horse allergy under control, he took allergy pills. When he was out of town, filming, he'd bring his pills. He would travel to the nearest English-riding stable and learn from another trainer.

Unlike Western riders, Chris rode in the smaller English saddle. There was no saddle horn to hang on to. English riders sat tall in the saddle and held the reins with both hands right in front of them. They wore hard black hats to protect them if they fell. Riders even wore protective vests. They often needed them. Combined training was full of jumps and tricks and speed. Sooner or later, all the riders fell off. The danger only made it more interesting to Chris.

At home he got all of the equipment. He outfitted Dana and the children, too. They rode as a family for fun. Chris rode more seriously. He wanted to compete. Being Chris, he also wanted to win. He hired the best trainers

and bought the best horses. He could feel his skill growing.

His family was growing too. Dana gave birth to a son a year after their marriage. They named him William, but called him Will. Chris was thrilled. His marriage was solid, he had an exciting new hobby, and he was getting good acting parts again.

For an HBO film, *Above Suspicion*, Chris agreed to play a disabled policeman. In the story the hero had been shot in the back. The bullet smashed into his spinal cord and ripped it in two. Messages from his brain could not get to his body, and the policeman's arms and legs stopped working—he was paraplegic.

Chris had to learn how someone with limp arms and legs got into and out of cars. He needed to see how they were moved from a bed onto a sliding board and then into a wheelchair. He could read about it. But to play a paraplegic honestly, he had to get to know one. The movie producer talked to a rehabilitation hospital near Los Angeles. They let Chris come in and talk to a young woman.

A few months earlier she had been at home. An earthquake struck suddenly. A bookcase fell over and crushed her. Chris wanted to talk with her as he had with the veteran amputee years earlier. The woman could only cry. Sometimes she raged about her luck. Other times she cursed life itself. "The pain . . . it is hopeless. I want to die," she told him. Chris watched how helpless she was. His baby, Will, took just as much care—but Will would grow out of it. This woman never would. She was so depressed that Chris would leave in a sick, sad mood. "Thank God nothing like that ever happened to me," he said to Dana on the phone.

After the HBO film was shot, there were other acting projects. Then Chris went back to Williamstown for the summer theater again. He had a new horse, Eastern Express. Everyone just called him Buck. He was so smart and gentle, they could have called the big, light chestnut horse Sweetie Pie. He'd worked in combined event shows for ten years before Chris got him. They rode together every day. They practiced dressage. They worked over jumps. They galloped up and down hills together. Chris and Buck won several blue ribbons at horse shows in New England. Now, Chris felt, they were ready for a bigger challenge.

The season was almost over. Other riders from the stable in Bedford had signed up for a show in Culpepper, Virginia. Chris wanted to compete at a smaller show in Vermont. It would be cooler there. He had a hunch it would be a better bet for Buck and him, but the other riders talked him into the Culpepper show. That decision changed his life.

Dana, Chris, and Will drove down to

Virginia together. They checked into a Holiday Inn near Culpepper. Then Chris went to the barn to see if Buck was safe in his stall.

The morning of the race, Chris walked the cross-country course. Like all good riders, he needed to see the route first and do some planning. Chris paced off the number of steps Buck would have to take to jump clean and safe. He noted places where Buck might get spooked. He saw where he could make up some time and other spots where he'd have to slow Buck down.

Then he walked the course again.

Chris put on the fancy white dressage shirt and tight pants. He tied the fancy white scarf under his chin. Last came the formal black jacket. He tied his entry number on his back and the medical information tag onto his arm. It included his name, his doctor's name, what conditions and allergies he had, and who to contact if he were seriously hurt in a fall. Chris never thought he would need it.

He checked the row of tidy knots in Buck's mane. Chris mounted the horse and rode circles, warming his muscles up for the dressage event. Although Chris had memorized the course the night before, he reviewed it again in his mind. He could feel his tension rise as the time came for him to compete. Chris patted Buck's neck fondly. "We'll be fine," he promised.

At the sound of the bell, Chris urged Buck out of the starting position. He did it with his legs only. Pushing with one knee or the other, he took his horse through the complex pattern. The judge stood stiffly, marking down every tiny error. Chris tried not to think about that as he completed the course. His stablemates from Bedford clapped for him. "You did well!" they said.

Chris thanked them and hurried toward the barn. He had to undo all of the knots in Buck's mane. It should be flying free in the next event, cross-country. He changed clothes too. Cross-country riders wore colorful polo shirts. That way they could be identified from a distance on the large race course. Chris remembered his route and took a deep breath. He had only competed once at this level before. He and Buck would be facing jumps that were over three feet tall. They were to leave the starting gate at 3:01. He snapped his chest protector on. He buckled his helmet snugly under his chin.

They warmed up by galloping over three jumps, one after the other. The horse felt fine. Chris did too. Together they entered the starting gate.

The starter quietly counted down the time. "One minute," she said. "Thirty seconds." Then she counted down. "Three, two, one. Have a good ride."

Chris urged Buck into a wild gallop. They were going twenty-five miles an hour, and it felt like it. Chris grinned into the wind. The first fence came up. Chris lifted his bottom off the saddle at the exact moment Buck left the ground. The jump was three and a half feet high. Buck was very big and Chris was very tall. Chris's eye level was nearly twelve feet above the ground when they flew over the fence.

Buck landed soundly and Chris urged him to gallop faster toward the next jump. He wasn't worried about the second or third jump. After that, Chris knew, they got harder.

As he suspected, Buck cleared the second fence without a problem. They swerved to face jump three. It was a zigzag fence, the rails stacked in the shape of a *W*. Together they sped toward the jump.

As Buck was going to take off, Chris lifted his body.

Suddenly Buck stopped. He just planted his hooves in and refused to take the jump.

Chris flew forward. His body kept moving just as fast as Buck's gallop—but now there was no horse under him. Buck lowered his head so Chris's body wouldn't hit him. The horse's reins were still clamped in Chris's hands.

He flew through the air until the reins stopped him. Then he stripped Buck's bridle off and tore the bit from his mouth. Now Chris was flying in a great ark. People screamed from the sidelines. Chris's six-foot-four body dove toward the fence, head first.

He fought to free his hands. He *had* to stop the fall—to protect his head. But his hands were still tangled in the reins.

Chris's helmet hit the top rail first. His body drove on downward. With a sickening crunch, Chris's neck broke from his skull. The bones smashed his spinal cord. Then his body slammed into the ground so hard that it bounced. Chris couldn't feel that part. No feeling went up to his brain; no messages went down to his muscles. He tried to move. He tried to scream in fear.

Nothing happened.

Chris could not breathe.

"Call an ambulance!" someone shouted. "Help! Anyone?"

Somebody breathed into Chris's mouth. Sweet air flooded his chest. Chris blinked. An EMT kept breathing for him. Another kept talking to him. "Hang in there, buddy," he said. "Don't die. Don't die."

Chris could not answer. Tears dripped from his eyes. Too much was happening too fast. None of it made sense. Where were his arms? Where had his legs gone? He wanted Dana!

The ambulance siren screamed up near him. Chris could not turn his head to look. A tube was pushed into his throat. "Don't move his neck!" someone said, and cursed. "*How* can he still be alive?"

They wrapped a brace around his neck. They lifted him onto a stiff backboard. Someone gently moved his legs and arms onto the board. Chris could not move. He didn't even know what was happening. Later he learned that he was lifted into an ambulance. Someone kept breathing for him, squeezing air from a plastic bag down his throat tube. Chris lay still and numb.

"Find his wife, quick," a voice said. "This man is dying!"

The ambulance doors slammed shut.

Another Promise

Chris awakened slowly. *Where am I?* He could barely open his eyes. His head hurt. He could not move it. He closed his eyes and listened: the high beeps of medical equipment and a steady *whoosh, whoosh* beside him. *A hospital? Why?* Chris lost consciousness again.

It was days before he came to. He'd been rushed to little Culpepper Hospital. They put him on a ventilator there, a machine that breathed for him. From X-rays and scans, they knew his brain was fine—but his neck was badly broken. They gave him a shot to slow damage to his spinal cord. He was pumped full of pain medication and flown to the University of Virginia Medical Hospital. Nobody knew if he would survive.

After five days he woke up, frightened and confused. "Dana!" he yelled. He could feel his mouth move but no sound came out.

"I'm here," she said. She stroked his forehead. "Stay calm. You've been in an accident." She described his fall. "Do you remember that?" she asked.

"No." His mouth moved silently. Why can't I talk? Why can't I move my head? Where is my body?!

"Hush," Dana said. "Hush." She could see the terror in his eyes.

Chris relaxed a bit. If Dana was there, she would protect him. He wanted to reach for her. He willed his arm to move. Nothing happened. He had no arm. But he could feel Dana's fingers stroking his cheek. Chris held on to that.

"You are paralyzed," she told him. "Arms and legs, like a paraplegic. But there is more. You broke your neck right up at the second vertibra. That means your heart is still beating but you cannot breathe on your own."

That explained the constant *whoosh, whoosh* sound. It was a ventilator. Then Dana's words sunk in. *A paraplegic?* Chris thought. *Like that woman in California? Helpless? Hopeless?* I *am like that?* He felt tears trickle down the sides of his face.

"Chris." Dana waited until his eyes met hers. "They have to do surgery. I told them they needed your permission to do anything."

Chris bit his lip to get control. Then he listened as Dana explained how his head was being held so still. "The break was that bad," she said. Now Dr. Jane wanted to try to reconnect his skull to his spine.

"Dr. Jane?" Chris mouthed the words.

Dana read his lips. "Your neurosurgeon," she explained. "He is a great doctor."

A doctor moved into Chris's view. He knew the man from the few times he had drifted awake in the hospital bed. Dr. Jane explained in great detail what had been done. Metal pieces had been screwed into his skull. They were connected to a chain holding a big, heavy ball hanging beyond the end of the bed. "It holds the broken bones in your neck apart. Right now, your skull is only connected to your body by muscles and nerves and soft things. We can try to reconnect you—but there is only a fifty-fifty chance of surviving the operation. It is your only chance at living at all, Chris. Otherwise the slightest movement of your head could cut the rest of your spinal cord. Your heart would stop for good."

Chris watched Dana brush tears from her eyes. Then he felt her wiping his tears, too.

"Do it," Chris mouthed.

"First we need to suction fluid from your lungs," he said. "You have pneumonia. It could kill you."

"Do it," Chris said silently, looking at Dana. He ached to hold her—to tell her everything would be fine. But he could not move at all. He closed his eyes and heard the doctor leave.

Chris lay still thinking about what he had heard. He was a paraplegic. He would be a huge burden on everyone. He could never dress himself, never take a bath or go to the bathroom alone. He was completely helpless. Dana would have to do everything for him. That wasn't fair to her! They could never hug again.

Chris thought about his children. What kind of a father could he be for them? To never hold them again? Waves of sorrow swept over him.

And what was left for him if he survived the surgery? He would never ride horses again, never sail or fly, never bow while an audience applauded.

Chris felt tears on his cheeks. He had nothing left to live for.

Then he felt Dana's hands, warm and strong, holding his face.

"Maybe we should let me go," he mouthed. "Let me die."

Dana did not flinch. "Now you listen to me. I will support whatever you want to do, Chris. This is your life, your decision." Now she was crying along with him. "I want you to know that I'll be with you for the long haul, no matter what.

"You are still *you*," she said. "And I love you."

Chris heard the truth in her voice.

"This is way beyond the marriage vows," he mouthed. "We promised 'in sickness and health.' "

"I know," she said simply. There was no question to it. Dana would stay.

Chris knew the rest was up to him—somehow.

After a few shy peeks, three-year-old Will climbed on the bed. He snuggled beside Chris and kissed him. "I love you, Daddy," he said.

Matthew and Al flew to America to see their father. Gae came along. They all were overwhelmed by the room full of equipment it took to keep him alive for now. They patted his limp hand. They told him they wanted him to get well and said they loved him.

Now Chris knew he had something to live for: his kids. They loved him. They needed him. And Chris decided to be there for them, whatever it took.

The hospital set aside a whole wing for their famous patient. Every newspaper and TV station had covered his tragic fall. Now they called the hospital for updates. To save their switchboard, the doctors held press conferences. Then mail began to pour in. "Get well, Superman!" the cards said. Stuffed animals, flowers, posters, and balloons came by truckloads.

Visitors began flooding the hospital. All of Chris's friends wanted to talk to him. They thought it might be their last chance to see him alive. Chris's mother and father came. His brothers visited too. Aunts and uncles he hadn't seen in years stopped in. Dana's mother and father stopped by. His agent and publicity manager came. Other actresses and actors showed up to say encouraging things. Old school friends popped in. Everyone was sad and serious as they wished him well in his surgery. In one way or another they were all saying good-bye, too.

Then a strange little doctor in bright yellow scrubs bounced into Chris's room. In a deep Russian accent, he listed all the rude things he needed to do to Chris.

It was Robin Williams! Chris laughed for the first time since his fall. Robin and his wife, Marsha, stayed for hours. Robin clowned for a long time and then got serious. He asked how Chris was feeling. He took the time to read Chris's lips. He understood how frightened Chris was of dying—*or* of living. "If there's anything I can do to help, old buddy,"

Robin promised, "you can count on me. You know I love ya!"

Ten days after his fall, the doctors finally managed to cure Chris's pneumonia. He was scheduled for surgery.

The doctors put Chris's spine and skull together with wires, metal rods, and pieces of his own hip bones. It took hours. Then Chris had to start learning how to live as a vent-dependent quadriplegic. That took years.

"Try this now, honey." Chris's aunt Annie held a spoonful of mashed potatoes near his mouth. "The chef fixed it special for you." Chris had lost fifteen pounds after his operation. He hated hospital food. Even more than that, he hated being fed like a baby.

The chef at a local restaurant heard about the problem. "I'll fix food for Superman. I'll stay late. I'll come in early. I'll cook anything." And he wouldn't charge for it either.

It was hard, waiting to be fed. It made him feel helpless to have someone give him a sip of water. He squirmed inside, having to lie waiting for someone to scratch his nose. Being so dependent made him feel horrible. He felt incredibly thankful to those who were helping him, but he also felt angry and scared. Horror swept over him. Sometimes gratitude blossomed. Then guilt flooded in. What had he done to his wife? To his kids? To himself?

This wild roller coaster of moods went on all day. It was worse at night. Dana spent hours with him after Will had gone to sleep. "Read me a letter," he would tell her. "Take me away." Hundreds of pieces of mail came every day. Some people wrote of times they'd seen him on stage or in the movies. Others shared stories of their own illnesses. There were one-line cards and five-page letters from complete strangers. Old neighbors wrote with tales of Chris's childhood. Teachers wrote about their students' reaction to his accident.

And children sent greetings too. The letters gave him strength. He had not known he had touched so many lives.

A complete stranger had sent him a postcard of the Pyramid of Quetzalcoatl, a Mayan temple in Mexico. The more Chris looked at the picture, the more it meant to him. Hundreds of stone steps led up to the pyramid. At the top were puffy clouds and a sapphire blue sky. Chris asked Dana to tape the postcard on his heart monitor. He could see it from bed. When things got tough, he imagined himself walking up each one of those steps. Then he pictured stepping right off into the blue sky.

Most evenings, Dana sang to him, her clear pure voice soothing Chris's mind. Eventually she would have to leave for the night. Then there was only dark and the endless *whoosh, whoosh* of the ventilator breathing for him. His air came through a tube and down into his throat. The tube snapped onto the ventilator. The nurses taped the connection together so that the tube wouldn't pop off. Chris lived in fear of being disconnected from the ventilator.

It happened one night. There was nothing Chris could do. He could not yell for help or press a call button. He could not put the tube back on or call 911. All the air was gone out of his lungs and no more was coming in. Black terror fell over Chris. After he missed two breaths, an alarm sounded in the nurses' station. One ran to reconnect his tube. It only took moments. To Chris it seemed like forever.

After three weeks, Chris had to make a choice. The doctors at the hospital had saved his life. They could do no more for him, but Chris was not ready to go home. He and Dana talked with the doctors. Dana spoke with people from the American Paralysis Association. They helped her with solid information and calm advice when she needed it most. The Reeves decided Chris should move to the Kessler Institute for Rehabilitation in West Orange, New Jersey. Kessler was famous for helping people with disabilities. It was near their relatives. Dana found a hotel where she could live. She promised to visit him every single day.

"Here you are." A large black man in scrubs stood by Chris's bed. He was holding a glass of bright pink liquid. There was a long straw in it. "Now, we need to start getting weight on you, mon," he said. Chris recognized the nurse's tropical accent.

"The islands?" he mouthed.

"Yes, mon. I come from Jamaica. That is where I learn to mix fruit drinks." He stepped closer. "Everybody calls me Juice, mon. You too."

The nurse's quick cheerful talk and his wide smile made Chris relax. When he slipped the straw into Chris's mouth, the juice tasted wonderful.

"You see?" Juice did not give him time to

speak. "I tell you the truth. We learn many things here together, you and I." Juice let him drink as much as he wanted. Then he gently wiped Chris's mouth.

"Hoo, mon!" Juice teased when he raised Chris's blanket. "You be needing a shower tonight."

Chris froze. A shower? That meant getting out of bed! That meant taking his ventilator under water. What if his ventilator was disconnected in there? Water would get into his tube! He panicked. "No," he mouthed. "No, no, no!"

"All right then, big mon. I'll give you a sponge bath in bed. I shampoo your hair. And shave you too. Brush your teeth. You feel better."

Chris's temper almost blew. After all, he was a forty-two-year-old man, not a helpless baby. But Juice kept up a steady stream of cheery chatter as he worked.

"There now," Juice said. "All clean and shiny!" He smoothed fresh sheets and covers over Chris.

Chris had to grin.

"You make many friends on this floor, mon—people with troubles like you."

Chris felt his own grin die. He did not want to meet any of these other patients. Deep down inside he didn't feel that he was anything like them. He was glad he was alone in a room with just one bed. He liked having a guard at his door. That was to keep people out who wanted to get his autograph or get a picture taken with the famous Superman. It would keep overly friendly patients out, too.

Juice was gentle with him. He had seen this process before. Almost everyone refuses to accept terrible news when they first hear it.

"Let me tell you about your neighbors here," Juice said. "One little boy broke his neck diving into shallow water. A woman was in a car crash. An old stagehand fell off the lighting platform and hit the stage below. A surfer landed headfirst into the sand. Other folks had strokes and sickness. They all be in *bad* shape—but good spirits."

Another nurse entered the room and wagged her finger at Juice. "Shame on you, Juice! Keeping our famous patient all to yourself!" She turned to Chris. "I'm Janet," she said. "Time to turn you."

Chris was already used to this. There were real dangers to lying still for days on end. Wherever his weight rested on the bed, Chris's skin was pressed down—and hard. Tiny blood vessels were squeezed closed. The flesh stopped getting as much oxygen and nutrition. It could not heal itself if there were any cracks or scratches. And it could not fight infection. Pressure sores were a special danger for anyone like Chris who could not feel pain.

"Don't you be touching him now!" Juice scolded. "Chris been rolled back to front and front to back, scrubbed down and dried off."

"I've been turned so much I'm dizzy!" Chris joked.

"That's fine," Janet said. "You're safe—for now. We'll shift you every three or four hours.

Can't be starting any bedsores, now can we?" Chris ground his teeth. He didn't need anyone else to tell him how fragile he was! Everyone's big fear was hyperreflexia. If even something small went wrong with a quadriplegic's body, it could start a wild chain of nerve reflexes. They lead quickly to a heart attack or a stroke—and then to death. Chris would die. Hyperreflexia could be triggered by an infected pressure sore, or a too-full bladder, a sun burn, constipation, a pinch from exercise equipment. . . .

Chris would not feel any of those things happen. He would not feel his internal reflexes going hyper, either, until it was too late. That was why Chris needed nurses checking on him around-the-clock—and he always would.

Within days, Chris was ready to take a shower. In a week he got into a wheelchair. When he began meeting other patients in the hall, he was polite. Then he got to talking with them.

Soon he made friends. As he accepted their disabilities, he began to get used to his own.

At night he dreamed about skiing or sailing, the wind in his hair and Dana by his side. In the morning he awoke trapped in the horror of his life. Every morning he cried angry, sad, bitter tears. Then he looked at the Mayan temple postcard and calmed himself. Another photo had joined it on his wall. It was a photograph of the Earth taken from the moon. It was signed by every one of the astronauts who had been on that mission. "Nothing Is Impossible," it read.

"You religious?" Juice asked him once when he found Chris in tears. Chris shook his head. "Well, I am," Juice said firmly. "And I do believe you survived that fall for a reason. There is a purpose for you being here at Kessler. We just don't know it yet."

Chris remembered those words often. It made him think about how much good he had done with the Creative Coalition. *Is there anything I can still do,* he wondered, *paralyzed from the neck down?* It would be a real challenge. Deep inside, hope began to grow. Chris had always given back. He would again! For the first time since the accident, Christopher Reeve felt like himself.

His special electric wheelchair arrived weeks after he had been at Kessler. It was fitted to his body size and shape. To get into it, stretchy socks had to be pulled onto his legs. An ace bandage was wound tight around his belly. Those kept his blood pressure up while he changed positions. A bag to catch his urine was strapped to one leg. Next Juice or Judy pulled sweatpants onto him. They wrapped a wide foam collar around his neck, then dressed him in a T-shirt or sweatshirt and warm slippers.

Then a pair of nurses sat him up. If Chris's blood pressure reading was still fine, he was hoisted into the chair. His arms and legs were strapped into natural positions. The ventilator fit into a shelf on the back above the wheelchair's motor.

A plastic straw sat next to his lips. Chris could puff a little bit of air into it. He could sip air out of it, too. By changing how hard he sipped or puffed, he could make the chair roll forward or back, turn left or right. He could even change the chair's speed. Of course he ran into a piano, rolled over people's toes, and scraped walls before he got the hang of the puff-sip controls.

This meant such wonderful freedom! But Chris still wanted to walk. He *would* walk, no matter that he would be the first person ever to recover. He could turn his head now and feel pinpricks across the tops of his shoulders. It would all come back. He would *make* it come back.

He did a wide range of punishing exercises to keep his muscles ready for the day his spinal cord healed. So what if spinal cords had never mended before? *His would.*

To practice standing up, he was put on a tilt table. This machine swung his legs down and his head up. It moved very slowly so nurses could watch his blood pressure. At last he would stand six feet four inches tall again—not flat in a bed like a baby. Dana often came for this part of his exercises. She could stand beside him again and lay her head on his shoulder.

Before the accident, they had been planning to go to the Creative Coalition's annual fund-raising dinner. Chris wanted to go—even in his wheelchair. He had helped to start the Coalition. He had been its president, too. More important, he was the one who had asked Robin Williams to come and accept an award this year.

The doctors at the hospital said it was a bad idea. Chris, they thought, wasn't ready for this. But he talked them into it.

He was frightened. What if he drove his wheelchair off the stage? What if his bag leaked? Something might trigger hyperreflexia! What if photographers caught him in a

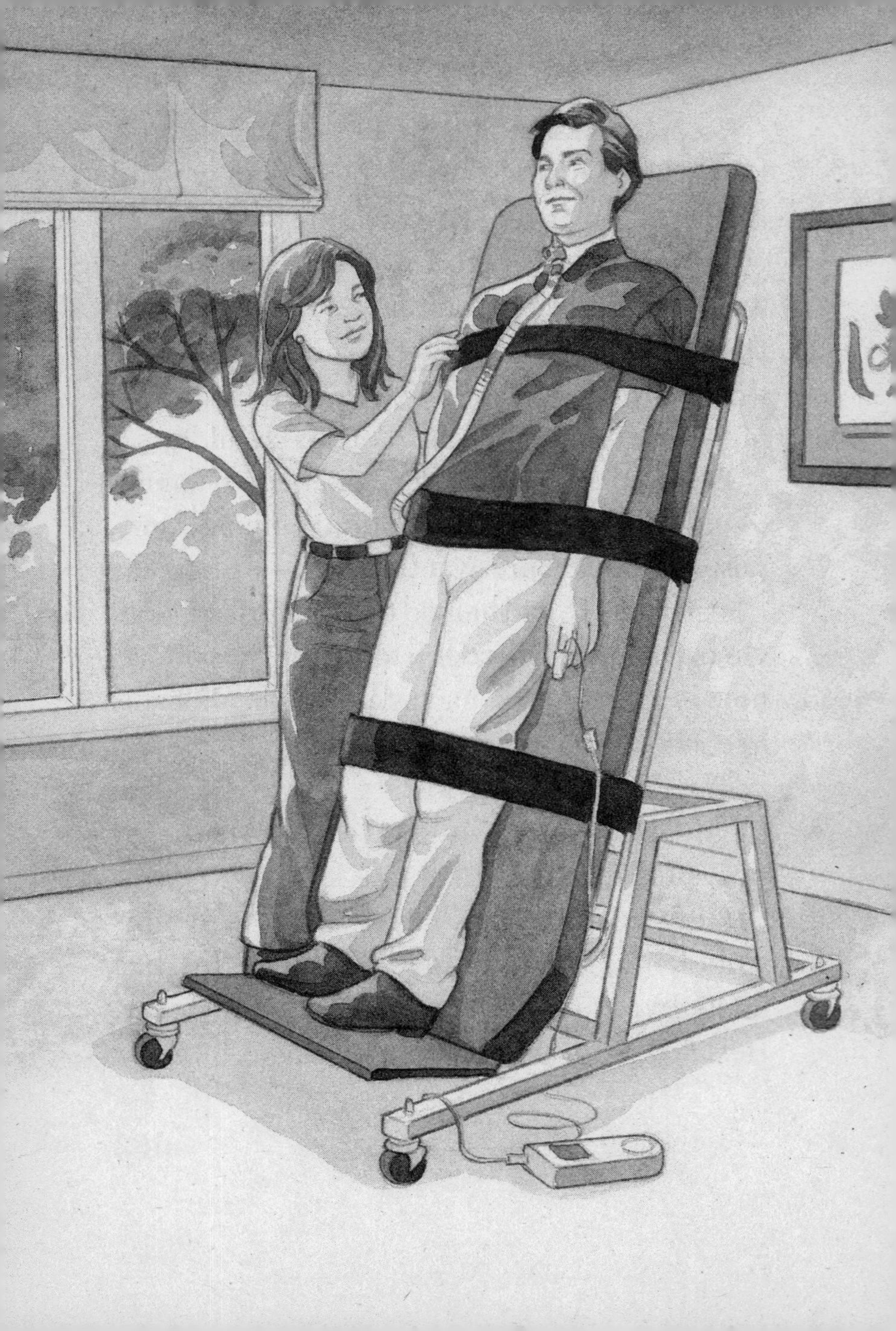

babylike state? Would people stare at him?

Juice and another nurse came along. Dana was there, too. Chris was driven to Washington, DC, in a van with tinted windows. He was shielded from everyone as he snuck in the kitchen door of the convention site. The chefs and kitchen crew backed up to let him pass, but they all applauded him. Chris hadn't heard that sweet sound in a long time.

Up the back elevator and onto the stage, and waiting for his cue to move, Chris worried. All the Coalition people used to be his friends—when he was whole. Would they just think he was a freak now? "Action!" a stagehand said, and winked.

Chris wheeled himself out into the lights. Everyone in the audience jumped to their feet to honor him. Their applause rolled on and on for five full minutes. Finally they sat back down. Chris realized he'd worried about everything—except what he was going to say. Suddenly he remembered his high school teacher, Mr. Packard. He told the audience about how even being a quadruple amputee was no excuse for skipping class. "So I thought I'd better show up tonight."

The audience laughed and Chris relaxed. He called Robin Williams up on stage with him. A few official photos were taken, then Robin began to clown around. He made fun of Chris's chair, of his air tube "necktie," and of his puff-sip control. Both Chris and the audience laughed together like old friends. They applauded Dana, and then Chris again.

After that Chris left quickly. He had to be back at Kessler by midnight, and he was exhausted. But he was elated, too. He wasn't helpless after all. He had done a good thing for his friend Robin this night. The audience was clearly touched by seeing him. He'd shown them that being a quadriplegic didn't mean you weren't still a person. And there was more. He had found a way he could help out a good cause.

The few photographs taken that night were sold the next day for a hundred and fifty thousand dollars. Chris gave every bit of it to the American Paralysis Association. They had been so helpful after Chris's accident. The APA could use the funds to help others.

Chris's mind boiled with ideas. Now that he had done this one event, he knew he could do others. He made a list of causes he still supported. He thought of people to call. He could not wait to get on with his life.

Within weeks he had found a staff of nurses to help him at home. Dana hired carpenters to put in ramps. A hospital bed was fitted into a first-floor room. The Kessler people wrote down the long list of exercises he was doing every day. A second ventilator machine was bought, in case the first one failed. There was so much to do!

Then finally everything was ready.

Dana and Christopher Reeve went home.

Superman, Take Two

Home. Chris had dreamed of it for nearly a year. He couldn't move into his old bedroom with Dana, though. His equipment wouldn't fit. And the old privacy they'd enjoyed with his family was gone. Chris needed a nurse and an aid on duty at all times. Some things were different, but it was home.

Chris could drive his wheelchair out into the sunshine on his porch. He could sit for hours watching the quiet countryside. The barn was empty. Dana had sold Buck and the other horses. Deer and foxes wandered in the fields now. It was beautiful. It was peaceful.

But Chris did not go home to relax. Besides the hours of care his body needed each day, he kept up a harsh schedule of exercising. "I *will* walk," he told anyone who asked. "I will." There was nothing wrong with Chris's muscles. He just couldn't send *Move!* messages to them down his ripped spinal cord. To exercise, his nurses used an electric stimulator to trigger muscle movement. He even pedaled on a special electric exercise bike. It shocked his muscles into moving the right way.

All of this equipment was expensive. Paying salaries to nurses twenty-four hours every day was expensive too. The insurance company said they would only pay for Chris's home care for a month and a half. After that, he was on his own.

Chris was horrified. He could not survive without help—lots of it. And what if the expensive equipment broke? Even with all his money, they couldn't keep going for long. He and Dana wrote many letters to the insurance company. He threatened to make a scene in the newspapers and TV. He could easily do that. He had been Superman. He had many important friends and many, many fans across the country. The Reeves finally convinced the company to make an exception for them.

Chris remembered his many disabled friends at Kessler. They did not have his kind of money. They did not have his fame, either. No one would listen if they spoke about their problems.

Chris decided to be their advocate. He fought with the insurance industry on behalf of everyone disabled by sudden spinal cord injuries. He wrote letters, called senators and congressmen. Now that he knew he could travel, he agreed to give speeches, too. The press covered everything he did. New insurance laws were written. Chris didn't get everything he wanted, but he had made a start.

With national attention on him, Chris decided to create a Christopher Reeve Foundation. It would raise money for medical research to help victims like himself. The foundation organized conferences during which researchers could swap news and plan new experiments. It would give grants of money to scientists who were making progress in spinal cord treatment. Many donors gave money immediately.

Within a year, he spoke at the Democratic National Convention. He talked of course about rights for the disabled. People listened to him. He lived what he was talking about. Also they all knew how much work it took for him simply to stay alive. They couldn't imagine the effort and energy it took for him to come and speak.

Next he worked on a documentary called *Without Pity: A Film About Abilities*. Simply by being himself, he made the point that handicapped people were just regular people—who happen to have a handicap. In 1997 he won an Emmy for his part in the movie. He got a star on the Hollywood Walk of Fame, too. People had loved him as a movie star. They had watched him overcome his horrible fate.

Now everyone respected him as a true hero.

What they didn't know was that Chris was beginning to breathe on his own. At first it was just a few breaths at a time. It was scary. It was uncomfortable. But he kept pushing. Soon he could go two minutes without his ventilator, then five. It made all the difference for his speaking. He could say a whole sentence instead of just one whoosh's worth of air. "Someday I will be off the vent altogether," he announced when he decided to tell the public.

By now Chris had acted in stage, TV, and film projects. He had always wanted to try directing. He had his chance with *In the Gloaming*. Chris sat in his chair in a room near the filming. He watched the action on a closed circuit TV. His voice was piped into the studio. Before Whoopi Goldberg began a scene, he could describe the effect he wanted to give the viewer. "Action!" he would say. He even got to say "cut!" if he thought Whoopi could try the scene a different way. Then he helped with the editing, too.

As the years went on, he began to have just a little feeling in his skin. It should not have happened. The doctors had told him it could not happen. Yet when Dana stroked his skin, he felt it. Best of all, when Matt or Will or Al gave him a hug, he could feel it!

Chris increased his exercises. If some spinal nerves had healed, they all could. He *would* walk! For his next creative task, he took on writing his own biography. He called it *Still Me*. Those words came from Dana's speech to him right after the accident. The book took years to write. He had to dictate it piece by piece to a secretary. To revise it, he listened to someone read it aloud. He made changes as he heard clumsy places. Then he and Dana went through family photographs, picking the best to include. They got photos from his schools, shows, and money-raising foundations, too.

Nerve doctors at the Christopher Reeve Foundation were buzzing with wonderful news. Research was showing that embryonic

stem cells could grow into any kind of adult cells. "They could grow into new nerves!" one doctor said. "They could be used to patch injured spinal cords!" Another scientist realized they could heal brain damage. A diabetes specialist said stem cells could be raised to cure diabetes. True, there would have to be years of research, but Chris was breathless with excitement. A cure! Not just for him, but for all the others. There could be a cure!

The foundation would finance a bit of that research of course. But the really big money would come from the United States Government. Chris wrote letters to every member of congress. He wrote to the White House. He gave speeches and wrote editorials for papers. The U.S. *had* to use these unwanted stem cells to save people's lives!

However, President George W. Bush announced that the government would only finance research with a few kinds of stem cells because of the controversial nature of the experiments. That sounded good at first, but many of those cells turned out to be useless. Chris was wildly disappointed. So were the millions of people whose conditions could be cured someday through stem cells.

Chris turned back to his art for comfort. He agreed to be in a TV movie. *Rear Window* was an old suspense film about a wheelchair-bound man who is under attack. Chris was worried at first that he could not act without moving his body. Then he saw some of the close-up shots of his face. All of his emotions showed clearly. Chris was feeling fulfilled. He was finding outlets for his creative urges.

He was also busy as an activist. He and Dana had found ways to help people who were facing sudden spinal cord injuries. Their families needed help, too, Dana always reminded him. Together they founded the Christopher and Dana Reeve Paralysis Research Center. The PRC office or website, www.paralysis.org, holds a storehouse of information for victims and their caregivers. "This is exactly what I needed when you were first hurt," Dana told Chris.

A new Superman spin-off was playing on television. Called *Smallville,* it told the story of a young Superman. To his delight, Chris was asked to appear on the show as the young boy's father. Fans wrote in by the thousands. Chris taped another *Smallville* episode.

He continued to raise money for the Christopher Reeve Foundation. Though he had nearly run out of his own money, he put every penny he raised back to research. After a speech for neurologists, she showed one doctor a miracle. Chris could move one of his fingers! Somehow there was a complete nerve connection between his brain and his finger. He was healing. It had been ten years.

He exercised even more intensely. He managed next to raise his hand from the wrist. Presently there was a little movement in his foot. In a few months he could move his arm. Onced told patients there was no hope of improvement. Chris, by his single-minded efforts, had proven them wrong. He had given all spinal injury victims hope.

In a TV interview Chris admitted that he was getting older. "The more time goes by, the more I feel a sense of urgency and I can accept anything except for complacency."

He drove himself ever harder. Few quadriplegics live long lives, and Chris knew that.

He was getting more pressure sores now. On October 5, 2004, Chris spoke at the Chicago Rehabilitation Institute to bring attention and funding to their research program.

That night his nurse turned him. "Oh, dear," she said. "Looks like you're getting a bedsore here." She applied an antibiotic and bandaged it. "We'll have to watch this one carefully."

By the next morning, the bedsore looked red and swollen. By dinner, it was infected. Within a day, the bacteria had leaked out of the sore and spread into Reeve's bloodstream. His temperature rose and the nurse breathed the dreaded word "sepsis."

The doctor came immediately.

"We can care for him at home, can't we?" Dana asked. "That's what Chris wants."

"This means putting Chris on an IV. That is the only way to treat sepsis. Two strong antibiotics will drip into Chris's veins. That should kill the bacteria in his blood, but it should be done in a hospital."

For a few days, the medicine seemed to be working. Hyperreflexia was the worry on everybody's mind. Even the irritation of the needle in Chris's vein could set it off.

Reeve was at home when he suddenly fell into a deep sleep. His nurse called 911 and the EMTs raced in. "He's in a coma," one of the EMTs told Dana. "We need to get him to the hospital." Chris never woke up again. His heart stopped and he died on October 10, 2004.

Chris's face was on the cover of magazines again. Everyone remembered his fame as an actor—and then his glory as an activist. He was given honorary degrees by Rutgers, the State University of New Jersey, in New Brunswick, and by Stony Brook University in New York.

Dana Reeve died of lung cancer less than two years after her husband.

Chris and Dana will be remembered by the children they left behind—Will, Matthew, and Alexandra—and their thousands of fans all over the world.

The Christopher Reeve Foundation continues to support research, and the Christopher and Dana Reeve Foundation provides information and support to hundreds of accident victims every month. Chris starred as Superman and then *became* a superhero, living a life of hope and determination that inspires everyone who learns his story.

CHRISTOPHER REEVE TIME LINE

1952 September 25, Christopher Reeve born
1956 Chris's parents divorce; he moves to Princeton, New Jersey
1961 Plays role in *The Yeoman of the Guard* for Princeton's professional theater
1967 Summer apprentice at Williamstown Theater Festival in Massachusetts
1974 Attends Cornell University
1974 Plays Ben Harper in the TV soap opera *Love of Life*
1975 Attends Juilliard School of Drama where he becomes friends with Robin Williams
1976 In Broadway play *A Matter of Gravity* with Katharine Hepburn
1978 Plays Superman in *Superman*
1979 Gae Exton, his girlfriend, has son, Matthew Reeve
1981 Stars in *Superman II*

1983 Gae Exton has daughter, Alexandra Reeve; stars in *Superman III*
1987 Travels to Chile to support seventy-seven condemned actors and directors
1987 Chris and Gae Exton break up
1987 Stars in *Superman IV: The Quest for Peace*
1992 April 11, marries Dana Reeve
1993 Dana gives birth to Will Reeve
1995 Plays paralyzed police officer in HBO's *Above Suspicion*
1995 May 27, thrown from horse and paralyzed
1996 Speaks at the Democratic National Convention
1997 Wins an Emmy for *Without Pity: A Film About Abilities*
1997 Gets star on the Hollywood Walk of Fame
1997 Directs *In the Gloaming*, starring Whoopi Goldberg
1998 Publishes his autobiography, *Still Me*; stars in a television movie remake of *Rear Window*
2000 Falls from wheelchair, breaks leg
2002 Christopher and Dana Reeve Paralysis Resource Center is founded
2003 In the TV series *Smallville*

2004 October 9, goes into a coma after a pressure wound leads to sepsis
2004 October 10, dies at Northern Westchester Hospital, after cardiac arrest
2005 Honorary degrees awarded by Rutgers, the State University of New Jersey, in New Brunsick, and Stony Brook University in New York
2006 March 6, Dana Reeve dies of lung cancer

For More Information

BOOKS BY CHRISTOPHER REEVE

Reeve, Christopher. *Nothing Is Impossible: Reflections on a New Life*, New York: Random House, 2002. Includes many of his important speeches as well as autobiographical information.

Reeve, Christopher. *Still Me*, New York: Random House, 1998. Christopher's life story. Includes black and white photos of family, plays, movies, wheelchair, politics.

BOOKS ABOUT CHRISTOPHER REEVE

Abraham, Philip. *Christopher Reeve* (Real People Series), New York: Scholastic, 2002. (picture-book, ages 5–7)

Hughs, Libby. *Christopher Reeve*, iUniverse, Inc., 2004. (ages 8–12)

ON THE INTERNET

www.christopherreeve.org, Christopher Reeve Foundation

www.Chrisreevehomepage.com, Christopher Reeve Homepage
Great information, many links to movies, reviews, photos, and a biography.

www.Kessler-rehab.com, Kessler Institute for Rehabilitation
This site demonstrates the incredibly complex care needed after spinal cord injuries.

www.nea.gov, National Endowment for the Arts

www.paralysis.org, The Dana and Christopher Reeve Paralysis Resource Center
This site has an interesting section for paralyzed children.

www.thecreativecoalition.org, The Creative Coalition

www.supermantags.org, CRF fund-raiser site with interesting stories

Acting Credits

Christopher Reeve worked steadily in many formats. There was not room in this book to cover all of his TV shows, movies, and plays, but this list gives an idea of how energetic, professional, and successful he was as an actor.

FILM

Village of the Damned, John Carpenter, director
Speechless, Ron Underwood, director
Above Suspicion, Steve Schacher, director
Remains of the Day, James Ivory, director
Noises Off, Peter Bogdanovich, director
Morning Glory, Steve Stern, director
Switching Channels, Ted Kotcheff, director
Superman IV, Sidney J. Furie, director
Street Smart, Jerry Schatzberg, director
The Aviator, George Miller, director
The Bostonians, James Ivory, director
Superman III, Richard Lester, director
Monsignor, Frank Perry, director

Deathtrap, Sidney Lumet, director
Superman II, Richard Lester, director
Somewhere in Time, Jeannot Szwarc, director
Superman, Richard Donner, director
Gray Lady Down, David Greene, director

TELEVISION

Rear Window, ABC
Black Fox, CBS miniseries
Sea Wolf, TNT movie of the week
Mortal Sins, USA Network movie of the week
Tales from the Crypt, HBO
Death Dreams, Lifetime
Bump in the Night, CBS movie of the week
Road to Avonlea, guest star on Disney Channel series
The Road from Runnymede, PBS/Constitution Project
Carol and Company, guest star on series
The Rose and the Jackal, TNT
The Great Escape: The Untold Story, NBC movie of the week
Last Ferry Home, WCTV-Boston/Hearst Entertainment

Anna Karenina, CBS
The American Revolution, PBS series
Love of Life, CBS series

THEATER

Broadway Theater
The Marriage of Figaro
Fifth of July
A Matter of Gravity

London Theater
The Aspern Papers

Off-Broadway Theater
The Winter's Tale
My Life

Regional Theater
The Guardsman
Death Takes a Holiday
Love Letters
Richard Cory
The Greeks

Summer and Smoke
The Cherry Orchard
The Front Page
Camino Real
Holiday
The Royal Family
John Brown's Body
Troilus and Cressida
The Way of the World
The Firebugs
The Plow and the Stars
The Devil's Disciple
As You Like It
Richard III
The Merry Wives of Windsor
Love's Labor's Lost
South Pacific
Fininan's Rainbow
The Music Man
Galileo

★★★ Childhood of Famous Americans ★★★

One of the most popular series ever published for young Americans, these classics have been praised alike by parents, teachers, and librarians. With these lively, inspiring, fictionalized biographies—easily read by children of eight and up—today's youngster is swept right into history.

ABIGAIL ADAMS ★ JOHN ADAMS ★ LOUISA MAY ALCOTT ★ SUSAN B. ANTHONY ★ NEIL ARMSTRONG ★ ARTHUR ASHE ★ CRISPUS ATTUCKS ★ CLARA BARTON ★ ELIZABETH BLACKWELL ★ DANIEL BOONE ★ BUFFALO BILL ★ RAY CHARLES ★ ROBERTO CLEMENTE ★ CRAZY HORSE ★ DAVY CROCKETT ★ JOE DIMAGGIO ★ WALT DISNEY ★ AMELIA EARHART ★ THOMAS A. EDISON ★ ALBERT EINSTEIN ★ HENRY FORD ★ BENJAMIN FRANKLIN ★ LOU GEHRIG ★ GERONIMO ★ ALTHEA GIBSON ★ JOHN GLENN ★ JIM HENSON ★ HARRY HOUDINI ★ LANGSTON HUGHES ★ ANDREW JACKSON ★ MAHALIA JACKSON ★ THOMAS JEFFERSON ★ HELEN KELLER ★ JOHN FITZGERALD KENNEDY ★ MARTIN LUTHER KING JR. ★ ROBERT E. LEE ★ MERIWETHER LEWIS ★ ABRAHAM LINCOLN ★ MARY TODD LINCOLN ★ THURGOOD MARSHALL ★ JOHN MUIR ★ ANNIE OAKLEY ★ JACQUELINE KENNEDY ONASSIS ★ ROSA PARKS ★ MOLLY PITCHER ★ POCAHONTAS ★ RONALD REAGAN ★ PAUL REVERE ★ JACKIE ROBINSON ★ KNUTE ROCKNE ★ MR. ROGERS ★ ELEANOR ROOSEVELT ★ FRANKLIN DELANO ROOSEVELT ★ TEDDY ROOSEVELT ★ BETSY ROSS ★ WILMA RUDOLPH ★ BABE RUTH ★ SACAGAWEA ★ SITTING BULL ★ DR. SEUSS ★ JIM THORPE ★ HARRY S. TRUMAN ★ SOJOURNER TRUTH ★ HARRIET TUBMAN ★ MARK TWAIN ★ GEORGE WASHINGTON ★ MARTHA WASHINGTON ★ LAURA INGALLS WILDER ★ WILBUR AND ORVILLE WRIGHT

★★★ Collect them all! ★★★

THE CALL OF THE WILD
by Jack London
Foreword by Gary Paulsen
0-689-85674-1

HEIDI
by Johanna Spyri
Foreword by Eloise McGraw
0-689-83962-6

THE RAVEN AND OTHER WRITINGS
by Edgar Allan Poe
Foreword by Avi
0-689-86352-7

A CHRISTMAS CAROL
by Charles Dickens
Foreword by Nancy Farmer
0-689-87180-5

PETER PAN
by J .M. Barrie
Foreword by Susan Cooper
0-689-86691-7

ANNE OF GREEN GABLES
by L. M. Montgomery
Foreword by Katherine Paterson
0-689-84622-3

A LITTLE PRINCESS
by Frances Hodgson Burnett
Foreword by Nancy Bond
0-689-84407-7

UNCLE TOM'S CABIN
by Harriet Beecher Stowe
Foreword by
Christopher Paul Curtis
0-689-85126-X

CHILDHOOD OF WORLD FIGURES

CHRISTOPHER COLUMBUS

ANNE FRANK

DIANA, PRINCESS OF WALES

POPE JOHN PAUL II

LEONARDO DA VINCI

MOTHER TERESA

GANDHI

THE BUDDHA

COMING SOON:

MARIE CURIE

★ ★ COLLECT THEM ALL! ★ ★